YOU'RE NOT DEAD YET

YOU'RE NOT DEAD YET

HOW GRIEF AND LOSS CAN TEACH YOU TO LIVE

DAVID FERRUGIO

JOSSEY-BASS™
A Wiley Brand

Published by John Wiley & Sons, Inc., Hoboken, New Jersey.

Library of Congress Cataloging-in-Publication Data:

Names: Ferrugio, David author
Title: You're not dead yet : how grief and loss can teach you to live / David Ferrugio.
Description: [San Francisco, California] : Jossey-Bass, [2026]
Identifiers: LCCN 2026022813 (print) | LCCN 2026022814 (ebook) | ISBN 9781394358533 cloth | ISBN 9781394358557 adobe pdf | ISBN 9781394358540 epub
Subjects: LCSH: Grief
Classification: LCC BF575.G7 F474 2026 (print) | LCC BF575.G7 (ebook)
LC record available at https://lccn.loc.gov/2026022813
LC ebook record available at https://lccn.loc.gov/2026022814

Cover Design: Jon Boylan
Cover Image: © Diane/stock.adobe.com
Author Photo: Liam Luxon

SKY10162221_071426

For my father, who left early.
For those still here, learning how to stay.

And for my mother and sisters. I love you.

CONTENTS

AN INTRODUCTION OF SORTS ix

CHAPTER 1
THE AFTERMATH 1

CHAPTER 2
ACCIDENTAL HEALING 7

CHAPTER 3
GRIEF GRAVITY 13

CHAPTER 4
THE POWER OF PERMISSION 33

CHAPTER 5
LOSS AS A GAIN 45

CHAPTER 6
WHERE THE GOLD IS 55

CHAPTER 7
AFTER THE GOLD 67

CHAPTER 8
LIFE IS A DARK COMEDY 75

CHAPTER 9
OTHER VIEWS 89

CHAPTER 10
WHILE WE'RE ALIVE 99

CHAPTER 11
WHEN WE DIE 115

CHAPTER 12
IT'S OKAY TO KNOW NOTHING 137

CONCLUSION
HEY, KID 153

ACKNOWLEDGMENTS 161

ABOUT THE AUTHOR 165

AN INTRODUCTION OF SORTS

"To realize that a purpose of human life, no matter who is controlling it, is to love whoever is around to be loved."
—Kurt Vonnegut, *The Sirens of Titan*

Let's get one thing straight: This isn't a book about death.

It's a book about life—which is impossible to talk about without running straight into the thing we spend most of our lives trying to avoid: death.

It's pitched to us that life and death are two neat categories like *clean laundry* and *dirty laundry*. But they're not. They're more like a pair of socks that somehow end up fused together in the dryer, and on folding our clothes we can't find the matching sock. You think you're dealing with one, and the other shows up anyway.

One version of my life ended on September 11.

And another began on September 12.

This was my wake-up call. I was 12 years old when my father was killed in the World Trade Center on the 105th floor. Before that day, my biggest question was, "Why does that kid have hair under his armpits?"

One moment, life was simple. And in the next moment, grief moved in like an uninvited houseguest that insists on staying forever. The kind that eats the food in your cabinet, rearranges your furniture and makes you question yourself in your own home. And yet, somehow teaches you things you didn't ask to learn.

But I didn't understand any of that then. I had inklings. But, not at 12. Back then, grief felt like a foreign object lodged down my throat. Congesting my ability to breathe. Confusing. Shocking. And absurd—which is a theme I'll come back to in later chapters.

Grief feels like every emotion, everywhere, and everything all at once. But here's the strange part: it's also one of the greatest teachers I ever had. I don't love its tactics, but they're effective.

Grief didn't just teach me something; it taught me everything.

And I won't pretend these lessons justify the pain. But they can give it a different meaning. If you handed me a receipt for my grief, I'd walk it right to the returns desk and get my father back in exchange for all that I've learned. But we don't get that option. So, we're left with perspective. And, if we want, a bit of meaning.

Grief has taught me that life is absurd, unfair, chaotic, and sometimes just plain dumb. Maybe we overcomplicate things because we're too busy trying to make sense of what it is, at its core, simple. And that sometimes the only thing that makes life feel "fair" is the fact that it's unfair to everyone.

If you've lost someone, you may know what I mean. Or maybe you don't. And, that's okay. Just because you're reading something in a book doesn't make it true. It's what you give it.

Death is a universal commonality. It binds us even when it separates us. And I also believe, in a strange way, it frees us.

THE SEED OF VOICES

Because my father was in the public light, I get text messages every year—texts, calls, acknowledgments, sympathy. Through that, I wondered about all the other people who died every day without the cameras and headlines. What about the ones quietly grieving behind closed doors?

Growing up, I wasn't great at expressing myself verbally. I internalized everything. I wanted to somehow express my emotions without using words. Turns out that's not how growth works for me, but I didn't know that yet.

For years, I avoided it with the outside world. Somewhere in my teens, I kept getting this cosmic whisper that I'd eventually end up speaking about grief with others. I didn't know why or how, but it felt tied to my father. Like whatever life had in store for me would start with him, end with him, or both.

In 2020 the whisper became a shout, when I finally launched *DEAD Talks*—a podcast meant to normalize conversations about grief, loss, and death. It didn't start out as it landed. First, I wanted to only interview comedians. Then I wanted to only interview people who'd lost a parent. Then I realized I was trying way too hard to curate a path that didn't need curating. So, I let it become what *it* wanted to be.

Death became the umbrella. And every raindrop—grief, love, fear, spirituality, science, identity—was welcomed.

Over the years, I've spoken with grievers, spiritual thinkers, scientists, veterans, parents, widows, atheists, believers, and people who have survived the kind of moments that split life into fragments. Somehow, every conversation left me more inspired than depressed. Inspired because even in unimaginable darkness, people found something—a lesson, a shift, and, dare I say, a sliver of meaning.

If you're looking for answers in these pages, I can't promise you'll find them. But maybe—just maybe—you'll find it within yourself to sit with the questions. To feel your way through the storm. To laugh in the silence. To cry without shame. To remember that amid all this grief and mystery, there is still life. And there is still you.

MY FATHER, SMALL THINGS, BIG REVERBERATIONS

I can still hear the clanking of metal where he'd throw around heavy weights. The endless slapping of a jump rope against the concrete. In a world where most of my friends' fathers were out of shape, my dad was jacked. And I absorbed this same discipline. I'm not saying I'm jacked but I'm not, not jacked. I look in the mirror now and catch glimpses of him—not just in my face or body type, but in the way I care about life.

One of my favorite memories isn't a typical memory—it's a feeling. He'd rush from work to make my baseball games. Sometimes he was late. I'd glance into the crowd before I'd throw a pitch or before an at bat to see if he'd arrive yet. And the moment I saw him?

That's when the game started for me.

His legacy wasn't one grand thing. It was a million tiny ones that added up to something enormous. My father, David Francis Ferrugio, loved the little things in life. I remember him weeding the lawn as a gesture of tending the metaphorical grass we walk on. He was one of those guys that when he came into the room you knew he was there. Not in a posturing sort of way but in the way he tried to make everyone feel at home. Whether it was his belting laugh that would reverberate through your spine or a belting fart that would send you running for the hills. He made life feel like it was supposed to. Being around him made me feel shameless, authentic, comforted, lighthearted, and present.

That's part of his legacy and what this book is about. The reverberations of death: life after loss and how it shapes us, how we live, and what we learn.

This book explores the lessons that we learn when we stop pretending loss won't happen to us, and what it might teach us once it does. The truths that surface when we face the fact that everyone we love—including us—will be *gone*, even though I don't think *gone* is the right word. I think death is a transition. I don't think we really die because I don't think we're just our bodies. And, even if you do think we're gone, the memories we hold keep our loved ones alive. But I'll save that conversation for a later chapter.

This isn't a guide. It's not a sermon. It's more like a road trip with an old-school Garmin GPS that occasionally shouts, "Recalculating!" Take what you want from this book—whether that's a little or a lot. I just hope it gets you thinking.

Let's normalize the conversation about death. If we're all going to die, we might as well figure out how to live.

But before I take you into the stories, lessons, and cosmic rabbit holes of this book, I need to take you back to where all of this began—not the day itself, but the moments before everything changed.

8:46 A.M., SEPTEMBER 11, 2001

I'm sitting here with economy leg room, high above the clouds, and it feels like the perfect metaphor for what grief does—it suspends you between worlds. I'm distracted by gargling snores from the man in 34C wondering if he even knows he does that. My attention is drawn to the man across the aisle tearing his paper into shreds. Maybe he's writing his first book, too.

And here I am in 56C, struggling to tell the story of my first "big death."

My heart flutters, my nerves jump, and there's an odd excitement as I begin writing this book. It's uncomfortable, and I like it. As much as my body rejects it, being uncomfortable excites me because I'm stepping into uncharted territory. And it feels fitting that I'm writing this book on an airplane, considering the nature of my story.

The usual white noise hum fills the cabin. Somehow it all becomes metaphorical of this life. We're all on this ride together in our own seat with the same final destination. Although there are many different flights, we all travel the same sky. We are all more connected than we think, even in our own sobering individuality.

Maybe that's life. Individual yet universal.

Maybe that's grief. And, it took grief to split me in two.

The first version of myself died on September 11, 2001.

That night was the last time I would see my father. I still see the image—my bare-chested father leaving the kitchen, then turning back to give me a small wave and his signature, "Good night, kid."

I don't remember my exact response. And the weird part is, I'm not even certain this memory was from the night before. But it's the memory I've kept, the one I've clung to as his last goodbye.

It was 9:00 a.m. on September 11, 2001. I was 12 years old and in seventh grade. It was first period. My friend Jeff, notoriously late for school, walked in and approached me with a question I'll never forget.

"Doesn't your dad work in the World Trade Center?" he asked.

"Yeah?" I said curiously.

"A plane flew into the building," Jeff said bluntly.

I was completely confused and didn't know what else to say except a whopping, "*What?*"

A plane? What does he mean a plane flew into my dad's building?

Perplexed and panicked, I headed to the main office to make a phone call to my mother—and they wouldn't let me.

Middletown, New Jersey, was a big commuter town for people working in Manhattan and the town that lost the most people in New Jersey that day. I now believe they wouldn't let me make a phone call because too many people were trying to do the same, and perhaps to avoid instilling panic.

Many years later, I would learn that my mother's decision to leave me in school that day was for a similar reason. She didn't want to bring me into the madness of the house, not knowing if my dad was still alive or what was happening. I imagine she was frantically trying to put the pieces together to understand the gravity of that morning. I stand by her decision. As well as just about everything she's done and continues to do for us. Rosanna Ferrugio is the epitome of what a mother is. To date, I exist in awe of the power of unconditional love that is pressed on me through this woman.

Nevertheless, I went through the entire school day in confusion, not knowing what was going on.

Kids were being called down to the main office one by one, and I kept wondering why I wasn't one of them. Clearly, something strange was happening, and my imagination ran rampant. My friends, seeing that I was worried, teased me about it. We were boys, and that kind of immaturity was expected.

I remember my friend Alec teasing me in the lunchroom. I don't think I really reacted but just absorbed his naive conjecture. The surprise comfort was from my friend Matt laughing at the joke yet simultaneously putting his hand on me as if to say, "It'll be okay." But it wasn't going to be okay for quite a while.

The rest of the day in school was a blur until the last school bell echoed as a vibrational transition to the next phase of my life.

THE WALK HOME

The last bell served as the last checkpoint of my childhood innocence. I walked home with my best friend James (who is still my best friend today). He was the quintessential troublemaker, and it just so happened that his misbehavior was one of the greatest gifts of my life.

He had gotten suspended from the school bus the year prior, a suspension that carried over into seventh grade. His mother asked my mom if James could walk home with me until the suspension was lifted so she could pick him up later. There's no one else I'd rather have by my side that day, on what felt like a long walk through the valley of the shadow of death and uncertainty.

I've asked James what he remembers from that day, and he recalled how quiet the walk home was. As if we didn't have the computing power to even imagine what was going on. And now it makes sense why I don't remember what we spoke about on the way home because it might have been nothing. Just a slow walking silence with every step getting us close to news that would shatter the quiet. It's the quiet idle moments that tend to be the noisiest.

The one thing he told me that stuck out the most was turning the final corner and seeing all the cars outside my house. And it was at that moment, I knew it wasn't good. Like a drop on a roller coaster, everything shifted within me with an unfamiliar knowing.

We walked into the house, where James and I were separated. I don't remember any words when I entered the house. This reflection feels like an old silent film where the visuals tell the story. I walked from the same garage door my father would walk in from five days a week after a long day at work. I turned left through the kitchen where we shared countless family dinners and into my living room where my shirtless father would enjoy his weekly fudgesicles. As I approached the living room, I saw my cousins sitting on the couches. They looked scared—not just for what I was about to learn, but for the awareness that their little cousin's life was about to change forever.

Their terrified faces foreshadowed the expression of my future.

I needed to see the TV.

Someone tried to block me as I walked into the living room, but nothing was going to keep me from it. I broke through, and there it was—the footage that would follow me for the rest of my life.

The plane.

The impact.

The fire.

The building my father was in.

It felt like *I* was the tower. Like the plane didn't just hit steel but struck straight through my chest. My heart exploded. My body gave out. I let out a cry so deep that everything went black. My system overloaded, the only defense my young body had against something no child could digest.

I don't remember the rest of that day. There's so much I still don't remember. The fog of forgetfulness became its own kind of grief. But I will never forget the walk home—the transition between two lives. One version of me died that day. Another one began the moment my foot hit that bend around the corner to my home.

The boy I used to be had left.

The man I would become hadn't arrived.

I was between worlds.

Grief has been everything between those steps—fog, shock, forgetting, remembering, love, pain and the processing of the fragments that eventually shaped who I became. A knighthood given without permission. A role I didn't understand but instinctively stepped into with the guidance of my family. My life split in two, the tide of realization washing in and out for decades after, succumbing to the unknown.

YOU'RE NOT DEAD YET

CHAPTER ONE

THE AFTERMATH

"You carried your father's love with you through everything you did. You didn't see it, but I saw it."

—My Mother, Episode 110

While I was staring at the clock, the Towers were burning.

While I was bored in first period, I think it was chorus, my father was dying along with thousands of others.

While I was imagining scenarios in my head, the real one had already ended.

Two parallel dimensions of imagination and reality.

Two timelines running at once.

By the time I got home and saw the footage, it was already over.

My mother was now a 44-year-old widow. Born from an immigrant mother, five brothers and sisters in Brooklyn with a backbone that was seemingly made to handle life's difficulties.

My oldest sister, Jacqueline, was now a fatherless 19-year-old. A young woman who wears her heart on her sleeve, beautifully pure and authentic.

My remarkable middle sister Gina was now fatherless at the tender age of 17. She's unmistakably smart, willfully strong, and just like Jacqueline she has a "no matter what, no matter when, no matter where" mentality for her family.

And I—12 years old, clueless, frustrated, observant, internalizing everything—was pushed into a world I didn't have the emotional vocabulary to explain.

Before 9/11, we were a tight family. But we hadn't been tested. Our swords were sharp, innately ready for battle, but dormant. And then the battlefield came to us.

I'll never forget a moment from earlier that year. My sister Jacqueline and I were shooting hoops outside. One of my best friends had just lost his father. Between dribbles we were reflecting on his father's death and had a solemn moment of imagining if that happened to us. Looking back on it, it was an eerie foreshadowing.

At that time, I didn't know my ass from my elbow. (And to date, sometimes I find myself sitting on my elbow.) I was just a boy. But fate shoved me into emotional puberty long before my time.

It felt as if I was given a new pair of glasses. I didn't even wear glasses, but my metaphorical old pair were ripped off my face, stomped and shattered. This new set of lenses gave me not only a new vision of the world but a new understanding of what it meant to feel. And, at times a new confusion of what it meant not to feel.

I'd see my childhood friends with their fathers at Little League games, doing what fathers do—showing up. My dad used to do that. It wasn't just the piece of my heart that was missing. Now I had a constant reminder for what the world looked like without a father.

When my friends would get frustrated with their dads like normal teenage boys, I'd silently boil. *How dare they get frustrated! Don't they know how lucky they are?*

However, the rest of my family showed up, enduring the boring baseball games. I realized I didn't have my father, but I still had my family and friends.

Even before I ever heard the word *grief,* I knew my sisters and my mom were going through their own hell. Two young women at the beginning of their lives now flipped upside down. My mother, now widowed, in the first week of a brand-new job having to raise a young boy and navigate the grief of her daughters. Even though we were tight-knit each of us was, at times, isolated in our own grief. We all process differently. Grief made us say: we're in this together . . . but also alone. Same house, same father, same loss, but four different griefs. Four lenses, four timelines, four ways of loving, losing, and surviving. And, at a young age the focus was my immediate family. What got lost in youthful ignorance was that my aunt lost her brother. My grandmother lost her son. My cousins lost their uncle, and countless others lost a friend.

My mother exemplified courage. Nothing stood in her way when it came to her kids. And, if you did stand in her way you were likely to get smacked by the literal and figurative wooden spoon. She had to endure the death of her husband, the aftermath of death, work, her girls, and her son who was easily frustrated. I was impatient with her. She did nothing wrong. Chalk it up to teenage angst . . . or the fact that my dad was dead. Probably both.

But I know this much: my family was and is everything to me. And even with that support, something inside me felt empty.

Someone once told me I was "the man of the house now." It embedded itself in my mind, quietly looping for years. Some say it was too harsh for a boy to hear, but I needed to see it that way. To me, it was reality. A challenge. I needed to be there for my family. It's a belief I still carry today. Besides, my father just died violently in front of the world so nothing was too harsh for me to hear.

The beautiful part is realizing my mother and sisters raised me into that man. I learned from a balance of strong, capable women and the substitute father figures who stepped into my life with quiet consistency.

In the immediate aftermath, my mother was on autopilot. Deferred her own well-being and focused on everyone else's. Captain of a ship who was kept afloat by love. We were the reason she didn't sink. Not because of the support we gave her—but merely because we were alive. And grief wasn't only emotional—it was logistical. Financial decisions. Legal procedures. Bureaucratic audits determining how much my father's life was "worth." Money she didn't want. Paperwork she didn't want. All while steering three children in three different emotional universes intentionally superseding her own.

It wasn't until decades later that I saw my father's death certificate for the first time. Pages and pages of documents in the same file cabinet—all things my mother had to handle while grieving that I was oblivious to as a teen. I realized then how little I understood about what she shouldered. How unaware I was of the worlds crashing around me and limited grasp I had of my family's experience at the time.

We went back to school a week later. My mother told me many years later she didn't want us to get "fucked up." Or perhaps "too" fucked up. After weeks of meals delivered to our home from our incredible support system, one of my sisters asked if she could make a home-cooked meal instead. On my family's podcast, my mom said that request made her exhale—because for an Italian American family, food is love. And in that moment, a plate of homemade food wasn't just love; it was normalcy.

At the dinner table, my mom created a space where we could talk—or in my case, sit in silence. She told me later that I would just sit there quietly and watery-eyed, absorbing our new reality. Hearing that as an adult reminded me of the path I've taken—from holding everything in to finding comfort in expression and vulnerability.

My childlike behaviors still surfaced. My brother-in-law—*my brother*—played video games with me in the den during the adult chaos. I thought he was just hanging out. Now I know; he was giving me a sanctuary—an outlet to still be a kid. A piece of normalcy in the abnormal. He was a male figure I needed in my life. He was there for me all the time—even to this day.

All of this—dinner tables, video games, homemade meals, quiet moments, tears—was my mother's mission. A reminder that amidst grief, we can still find joy. Amidst pain, we can still find solace. Our world had shattered, but the rest of the world didn't crack with us. Life didn't stop so we wouldn't either.

It felt like doing a puzzle in the dark. We had to blindly find which pieces fit, guided by something unseen, hoping for connection and stability. Unnatural yet completely natural at the same time. Intentionally accidental. But we had to start somewhere—even if that somewhere was in the rubble.

CHAPTER TWO

ACCIDENTAL HEALING

"Grief sometimes does not make you a better person right away. Grief sometimes is so painful that you are the absolute worst version of yourself."

—Nora McInerny, Episode 150

I accidentally found my way.

Then again, perhaps it wasn't accidental.

Maybe it was natural.

Or perhaps it wasn't natural but just an attempt at *something*—anything—that felt like control in a world that suddenly had none.

I came to believe that repeatedly watching the horrific footage of that day not only made me more "comfortable" with it (for the record, I'm not a sociopath)—it made me *feel*. It stirred something inside me that was still and numb.

The 9/11 footage began as an open wound. Later it became something else entirely. As a young teen in the following years, I'd kept seeking the footage of that day in search of an answer hidden in the smoke and debris. I wanted to see every angle of the plane striking my dad's building with such force that I could feel it. It felt sadistic, but really I was seeking understanding. It was an emotional attempt to get as close to the fire as my father was. I wanted to know what the thousands of others felt. I wanted to be there. I wanted to feel, and I wanted to cry.

By facing those images and replaying the worst day of my life on an endless loop, I wasn't torturing myself. I was teaching myself to bear the unbearable. To coexist with it. To stare directly at the most unimaginable thing and say, "I can still stand here. I can still breathe."

There's something about standing in the eye of the storm and realizing you're not being blown away.

There are two realities: the one we think we live in, and the one we create. Two parallel worlds, separated by an invisible boundary. As a kid, I unknowingly chose to blend the two. I let the event be just that—an event, one that didn't happen *to* me, but *around* me. And once the emotional intensity began to settle, I realized something unexpected: I was still here. I was okay.

I didn't know it then, but this was my first form of therapy: exposure. The kind psychologists write about. The kind that breaks avoidance by inviting you to face what terrifies you until it loosens its grip, even just a little.

Exposure therapy is a psychological treatment that was developed to help people confront certain fears. It's common to avoid what we fear whether it be objects, people, certain situations, or in this case, grief. The avoidance could help reduce certain emotions but over the long term it can worsen the fear or negative emotions. In clinical environments a "safe environment" is without danger in which to "expose" the patient to the source of the trauma. The exposure to the subject can help reduce the feelings whether it be anxiety or fear attached to "it" and decrease the running avoidance.

It is one of the most empirically supported treatments not only for trauma but also anxiety which often is a part of our trauma.[1] It's a mechanism that doesn't erase the fear that comes with facing these trauma-induced events. It's inhibitory learning,[2] a process by which exposure therapy can help the brain form new associations that compete with the foundational fears we associate our trauma with. It's not forgetting; it's rewiring a new understanding.

And, turns out this is exactly what I was doing. So, feel free to read other cited studies but I am here to tell you my own empirical evidence.

I hunted for every angle, every frame, every snippet of video. I studied the collapse of my father's building like a ref breaking down a replay—trying to see if both feet were in bounds. I didn't want to just *watch* it. I wanted to *feel* it.

I wanted to cry. I wanted to dive into the suffering. I wanted to be in the smoke, the chaos, the heartbreak. Beside my dad—or maybe, in some strange way, *in his place*. I used my imagination to create answers that I eventually learned would only come (and remain) in fragments. I learned that some answers come in the form of acceptance.

It forced me to *vibrate* with pain—sadness, anger, confusion—all of it, all at once. There was no room for distraction, no space for avoidance. I had to face my emotions directly, without flinching.

---

[1] Foa, E. B., & McLean, C. P. (2016). The efficacy of exposure therapy for anxiety-related disorders and its underlying mechanisms: The case of OCD and PTSD. *Annual Review of Clinical Psychology*, *12*, 1–28. https://www.annualreviews.org/content/journals/10.1146/annurev-clinpsy-021815-093533?utm_source=chatgpt.com.

[2] Abramowitz, J. (n.d.). The inhibitory learning approach to exposure and response prevention. International OCD Foundation. https://iocdf.org/expert-opinions/the-inhibitory-learning-approach-to-exposure-and-response-prevention/?utm_source=chatgpt.com.

And by confronting it head-on, I began to accept it.

It didn't just help me face my father's death—it helped me face the world. The discomfort. The vulnerability. The conversations that make your throat tighten. It didn't erase the fight-or-flight instinct completely, but it tuned me into something deeper: the ability to choose *presence* over panic.

I learned how to live and grieve at the same time.

And somewhere along the way, that choice—over and over again—began to dissolve the grip of that old, buried fear.

That grief oozed out of me—physically, mentally, and spiritually—even before I consciously stepped into the spiritual phase of my life. That exposure—facing my dad's death both ethereally and viscerally—was the beginning of my accidental healing process.

And then, I found another outlet.

Music and physical release.

Linkin Park's album *Hybrid Theory*—led by Chester Bennington—became my soundtrack. It was pain channeled through raw, unfiltered lyrics wrapped in a hard, aggressive sound. It was perfect for a moody, grieving teenager like me because it helped me unleash the rage I didn't know how to speak.

After school, I'd blast my record through my dad's old Bose speakers, slip on his boxing gloves, and face off with the punching bag hanging from the basement ceiling. As Chester screamed, I screamed. As the bass shook the floor, I hit harder. Eventually, I ditched the gloves altogether—punching until my bare knuckles bled.

It wasn't just noise or rage.

It was release.

I found comfort in the lyrics of someone else's pain because I realized that I wasn't alone. It helped me release all the pent-up energy that I couldn't verbally express. I found the clash of my knuckles to leather relieving. It seemed as though the bag was whispering to me to let it all out.

Not on its own, but as one element in a larger cocktail of healing that included physical release, exposure therapy, movement, and the support of my family.

And one of the most powerful ingredients in that mix wasn't something I did alone.

We have to do a lot on our own, but we don't have to do everything alone. My family was surrounded by people who showed up in ways we didn't know how to ask for—family, friends, and a community offering steady hands when words fell short. And when I stumbled, it was my sisters and my mother who caught me. Grief, I learned, is a balancing act: tending to it privately while also allowing others to help carry the weight. Learning not to be afraid of that support became part of the healing itself. And, finding support in ways that come in many different variations.

I came to realize that support wears many faces. Some people are fortunate enough to find it in personal relationships—others aren't. And when that's the case, the work becomes learning how to seek it both within yourself and beyond the people closest to you.

For me, support somctimes came from unexpected places. Hearing Chester Bennington pour his soul into lyrics, I found comfort in the voice of a man I never met. His pain spoke to mine. His scream gave mine permission to exist.

Support can come through community, through shared stories, through the words of strangers that feel eerily familiar. It isn't always your family or your closest friends—it can be a song, a book, a podcast, or a passing conversation that finds you at exactly the right moment.

And somewhere in all of that, I was becoming someone new.

Even as a teenager, even in the middle of all the emotional debris, I felt that split. The TV footage, the music, the release, the rage—these weren't just coping mechanisms. They were early molds shaping who I was becoming without my permission. And, at some point it became that permission that allowed a whole new life in.

I was criticized a lot for being indecisive—for not settling on what I wanted to do for the rest of my life. What I didn't realize then was that I had been reborn into a new purpose: to seek more, despite having no real understanding of what "more" even was. My indecision didn't necessarily mean I was discombobulated from the trauma or that I was lazy; it was curiosity. After losing my father as I grew older, I no longer believed in the "normal" path. What was normal about any of this? Why would I chase a blueprint when life clearly didn't honor blueprints?

The death of my father engrained things in me that wouldn't reveal themselves for decades. And, that's the delayed release of grief. It was an engine under the hood—one I didn't fully understand, but I trusted this undefined guiding force that was pushing me to keep seeking. I was driven, but by something invisible.

In a world of people focusing on what they want to do I found great value in understanding what I don't want to do.

And woven through all of this—the exposure, the punching bag, the grief, the search—was the challenge handed to me at 12 years old: **to be the support my family needed.**

Whether I lived up to it or not wasn't the point, even though it's something that I held on to for a long time. The point was that it shaped me.

My mother and sisters raised me into the man I eventually became. Jeff, my brother-in-law, showed me what showing up really is. The strong women in my life taught me that strength isn't tight-fisted—it's knowing when to lean and when to be leaned on and how everyone leans differently at the same time.

I didn't realize it then but my accidental healing wasn't just about getting through the pain.

It was the beginning of understanding who I was—and who I was becoming.

CHAPTER THREE

GRIEF GRAVITY

"What grief does, and what nobody sees coming, is it takes everything that you believe, everything that's right in front of your eyes, everything that your soul believes, and it turns it upside down."

—Matt Fraser, Episode 185

In July 2015, the unthinkable happened to Phil Cohen. His only son and his son's close friend were last seen leaving the Jupiter Inlet on a 19-foot fishing boat. Severe storms swept through the area, bringing heavy rains and winds up to 40 miles per hour. After multiple failed attempts to contact the boys via their cell phones, the Coast Guard launched one of the most extensive searches in its history. Neither of the boys was ever found, and the events of that day remain a mystery.

Austin Stephanos and Perry Cohen were just 14 years old when they vanished during a fishing trip they had taken countless times before. I'm not sure anything demonstrates the gravity of grief more than the death of a child. While I often feel there's no hierarchy of loss, there are deaths that carry a different weight—a gravitational pull—that seems undeniable. The death of a child is one of them.

I had the opportunity to speak with Phil Cohen, known for his powerful TED Talk titled "Transforming Grief: When I Lost My Only Child," on episode 44 of my podcast. This chapter may not be the feel-good part of the book, but it captures the raw reality of grief: the mind, body, and soulful impact. Phil's experience led him to develop what he calls *the grief continuum*, a framework for transforming loss into empowerment. But before transformation comes a lot of messy, unempowering gook.

Grief has a weight to it—one that doesn't just sit on your chest but pulls on your entire inner world. It bends time, distorts perspective, and changes the emotional physics you used to live by.

This is *grief gravity*.

Some losses reshape everything around them. They become a kind of internal force—one that shifts how you move through life, how you see the world, how you understand yourself. Time stretches. Minutes feel like hours and sometimes hours feel like minutes. Days disappear and simple tasks feel heavier.

The gravitational pull is different for everyone.

Some people fall inward.

Some collapse.

Some crack open.

Some grow stronger all on different timelines.

Gravity doesn't ask for your permission.

It just alters your center of existence.

And, once it does, you have to relearn how to live inside with a force that can tilt our axis.

And once I understood what grief gravity was, I finally recognized how deeply it had been shaping me. For instance, one of my biggest challenges was forgetfulness. It's as if my brain shut down due to the shock.

Recognizing that impact forced me to stop fighting grief as a single problem and start understanding it as something layered.

Through my own grief, I've learned to open my heart and mind to various angles of the equation—to see what works for me. I've learned from others but ultimately made my own decisions. Grief is a system of competing orbits—separate forces circling the same loss, occasionally colliding, never fully independent. I came to understand these shields as the ways we protect ourselves from feeling too much, too soon. They show up as distraction, forced composure, and the quiet performance of being okay when we're not. They help us function, move through the day, and survive the initial shock by covering emotions we don't yet have the capacity to face.

When I spoke with grief expert David Kessler, he reassured me how natural this response is—a protective mechanism designed to soften the impact of pain. But these shields aren't meant to be permanent. They're temporary by design. Eventually, they have to come down. In the immediate aftermath, my family didn't know whether it was better to keep our guard up, let it down, or live somewhere in between. Especially in the beginning, we had no idea what to do. Even among unknowingness I've found a current of primal knowingness that runs within us if we trust it. I don't know when I lowered my shield. But when I did, I gave myself permission to *feel*. And that's when I started to *feel* a little better.

That permission didn't just change how I felt—it changed how I listened to the world around me.

I've learned through the blackhole of internet comments that the notion of "it can get better" upsets people. I've been told countless times, *"It never gets better!"* But I disagree. It can get better. It doesn't mean we forget. It doesn't mean we erase the scar. It doesn't dishonor the person we lost. It means we grow around it. Like a tree struck by lightning, our bark thickens, and the roots remain intact. The charred wound is still there, but we grow *with* it. And, when you're in the thick of it, it's not always necessary to focus on the idea that it will get better because often that's impossible to comprehend.

Perspective has a way of arriving long after the moment that created the wound. In that we can grow, heal, and gain perspective—and still be left staring at the beginning thinking, *How the hell was this real?*

I was a boy then. I'm a man now. Still mostly a child, but I look like a man at least. And looking back on that day still blows my mind. A *plane* flew into my dad's building. Excuse my New Jersey French, but what the fuck?

The absurdity of the way my dad died just made me realize, *Oh, this shit can happen. And, oh, this shit can happen to ME!* As a man today who talks about death constantly this awareness has reduced my shock to life. *It doesn't fix the pain; it enhances acceptance.*

When life shows you how fragile it is, the philosophy of it all stops being abstract.

We all die. It's the most universal truth. Death has changed my life. It changes everyone's life and it's up to us to decide what that change will look like. Early on it was the acceptance of death as a part of life. And, when death becomes a constant companion, it's hard not to see the world differently.

My mother chose to teach me the lesson of not letting that Tuesday morning define us. We define it. She taught me that our response is a choice even when what happens is not.

And over time, death stopped being just something that happens—it became something that taught me.

Even with plenty of support it was me versus me. Part of my journey was learning to let go of the guilt that came with the attention I received—both within my circle and publicly. I eventually absorbed the fact that so many people don't have a fraction of the help I had, which is part of my why in creating this book.

Death isn't a surprise. Even when it shows up in the most unthinkable, gut-wrenching ways, I can't help but believe there's something woven into it—a thread of meaning stitched into the incomprehensible fabric of our existence. Not in the eye-roll-inducing "everything happens for a reason" kind of way . . . but maybe *kind of.* Maybe there's a reason. Maybe there isn't. I will tell you there is a reason if we give it one.

Exploring death, talking about it, sitting beside it has revealed a truth I never expected. That existence is wildly mysterious, terrifyingly beautiful, and filled with endless possibilities. I've come to believe that the discomfort, the sharp edges of pain, and the hollow silence of loss aren't just random suffering—they're teachers. They're where the gold is buried. And the gold is found in the seeking and dancing with the unknown.

The death of my father taught me to loosen my grip on life and to not take everything so seriously. Impermanence isn't a flaw in the system—it's the system.

If there's a practical joke in the universe, it's not that things end; it's that we spend so much energy pretending they won't. The punchline is our fear when reality finally reminds us. Once I stopped resisting that truth, my posture toward life changed.

Instead of running from death, I learned to dance with it—to let it sharpen my attention, not dull it. Death became a gateway, a way of seeing the world as more fragile, more fleeting, and therefore more precious.

And that shift carried me further than answers ever could. The deeper I've gone into the grief of losing my father—through my own lens, through my mother's, my sisters', my friends', and through hundreds of conversations about near-death experiences, the afterlife, philosophy, and everything in between—the less I *know*.

But I do know what I *feel*.

That life isn't about where we end up. It's pushing the stone up the hill without any guarantee that we'll make it to the top. It's a life filled with no guarantees and it's in the trying, the seeking that gives life its meaning.

That struggle isn't unique to me. It's part of the human condition.

What intrigued me most was observation—paying attention to my surroundings and the people moving through them. And the more I noticed, the more aware I became of how often I felt like the odd man out.

Because my version of that struggle looked different. I wasn't surrounded by a bunch of 12-year-old boys, let alone teenagers that didn't have their father. Except for my friend Scott, who lost his father shortly before mine.

It was as if no words needed to be said because there was an invisible tip of the cap every time we hung out. We got along prior to losing our dads, but afterward, there was a bond of understanding. Despite the difference in loss, it was relating to someone else outside of my family that made me feel less like a black sheep.

And, I found my shepherds within the community of people who were already part of my everyday life.

After my father died, I had multiple male figures step up in my life, and they understood that they would never be my dad, which was never the point. My brother-in-law, Jeff, was one of them. We were neighbors on Staten Island, and I've known him since the day I was born, long before he fell in love with my sister, the girl next door. And he did this just by showing up. No grand gestures or talks about the birds and the bees or how to shave. Just simply showing up, and to me that's what men do.

My second family became the boys and parents who were part of my Little League baseball teams. Stitching HK on our jerseys representing what my father was known for in saying "Hey, kid" to everyone he saw. How beautiful of a gesture to thread a couple of letters in memory of my father when it felt our world was just hanging by a thread.

Baseball was a shared experience with my father. There's the starting pitcher that opens the game. The go-to person. Sometimes pitchers can complete the entire nine innings of a baseball game, and other times, they need backup. That's when the bullpen is tapped and the relief pitchers come in. Simply put, I had a hell of a bullpen and whether your bullpen is one person, one hundred, we need them.

And the bullpen of my life never fully replaces the starting pitcher but they can guide you through the rest of the game. For me the game was growing up without my starting pitcher. It was going to prom with a girl

I liked and not having my father to pitch me some fatherly advice. After throwing my graduation cap to the clouds my dad wasn't there to congratulate me. Dad wasn't there to say, "Way to go, kid."

As I grew up I felt like I needed answers to why I felt "lost" and uncertain about what the rest of my life would look like. From my viewpoint, it seemed like my peers had more clarity about the future. Over time, I realized answers weren't what I was actually searching for. I've come to resonate more with emotion than answers. And all of it—this search, this exploration—has led me down a path toward love. Not just wanting and receiving it but giving it.

And, it's in the giving that makes me feel more a part of it all.

I've come to believe that this life is just a single thread in a much bigger fabric—some eternal quilt that's meant to keep us warm. But man, sometimes that quilt feels cold as shit. And in those moments, I question everything all over again.

Maybe the point isn't to resolve those questions, but to learn how to sit with them and allow the questions to guide us.

I have thoughts and you'll read more of them here. But the question I keep returning to isn't *What's the answer?* But *How do these questions affect the way I live?*

Not with the need for an answer but just a need for thinking and correlating those thoughts to how you live your life.

The aftermath of my big loss has made me want to ask questions, to share stories, to be open-minded and decide for myself. This often-unorthodox view of life I have all stems from death. But I'm grateful for my evolving perspectives and all that I still have to learn.

As a man today I still find myself learning from the younger version of myself.

I like the idea of experiencing life the way my younger self did—sitting at the dinner table, quietly taking it all in. Sometimes I'd cry. Often, I laughed. Sometimes I'd speak. But often, I simply observed. I'd watch the world move around me and try to make sense of it. Maybe my younger self knew then what I know now: that there's no sense to be made and it's all in the trying. What I didn't realize then was that I was practicing something. And maybe that's what life really asks of us: not always to act, not always to speak, but to stay aware. Because in awareness, we begin to see the world not just for what it is, but for what it can become. And what it becomes is up to us.

I know people who never "recovered." They remained metaphorically curled up in that dark room, unable to find (or even allow) a reason to keep going. But before that reason emerges, we must wade through the circus of emotions that grief brings.

Most people have heard of the five stages of grief. I later learned that Elisabeth Kübler-Ross originally wrote about these stages in the context of terminally ill patients facing their own mortality. Most people I've spoken with who've experienced loss don't move through grief in this orderly fashion. It's a chaotic mess—a nonlinear roller coaster. You might feel denial, then anger, then acceptance, then back to anger. You might skip stages entirely. You might revisit them years later.

Phil Cohen described his experience with grief as deeply personal and nonlinear. "For me, I almost felt like I was doing something wrong because I didn't experience grief like that at all. I sought counseling, talk therapy, EMDR [eye movement desensitization and reprocessing] therapy—and while they were helpful, none of them took away the pain. And honestly, I don't think the pain will ever fully go away."

He realized that grief isn't a school curriculum. We don't all start at the same place, graduate through neatly defined stages and emerge at a tidy endpoint. Grief is unique. It's shaped by our relationships, our upbringing, our life experiences and even where we are in life when loss happens.

You might feel all five stages. You might feel none. And that's okay. There's no "right" way to grieve. I think a lot of self-help books and even grief literature create this illusion that grief has a formula when it doesn't.

One example from a past guest, author, and a therapist who specializes on grief—Claire-Bidwell Smith—stood out after she explained to me that she couldn't even cry, which she says tends to confuse a lot of people. "I felt very shocked by her death even though she'd been sick for a long time. I just was really unprepared to lose my mom. . . . I didn't even cry for like a year because I couldn't even wrap my head around the fact that I was going to live a life without my mom. And so, when that finally began to seep in, then I cried for like five years."

What these frameworks can offer are references—signposts to help you explore your own grief. These frameworks aren't something we follow; they're something we uncover—buried in our awareness, revealed as we pay attention to what grief is already doing to us. All that we feel and are experiencing. They aren't rules. There are no shoulds or shouldn'ts. Okay, maybe there are: don't down a fifth of vodka every night for six months straight. And if you do, please don't drive.

The gravity of grief can feel like it's pinning you down, keeping you trapped. But at some point, we face a choice: do we let that gravity crush us or do we let it become the foundation for a new way of living? Regardless, it's going to be a new way of living so you might as well do it on your terms.

When I lost my dad at a young age, my response from his death often manifested as anger and frustration. And, sometimes it was that punching bag that became my outlet. There were times I wanted to take that anger out on someone else, but I held back. At some point, I thought I had accepted my dad's death. And yet, decades later, I still find myself questioning if the times I feel sad are stemming from my childhood grief.

I've often wondered how deeply engrained my trauma is. I catch myself pointing to parts of my life I want to improve and wondering, *Is it because my dad died?* Intimacy is one example. In relationships, I've found myself with one foot in and one foot out. Emotionally shut off, yet simultaneously expressive. I've always felt I could be more verbally open when it comes to love. Maybe I just haven't found the right person. Or maybe it *is* me—maybe I'm scared to lose someone because my dad "left me," and the deep-rooted trauma hasn't been reconciled. The emotional toll of losing my father—and the way I lost him—must have messed me up. I know it has. But maybe I don't fully understand the full effects behind it.

Death has rewired me—it's not just in my mind but in my body.

GRIEF IN THE BODY

What surprised me most was realizing through my own experiences and the hundreds of people I've spoken to is that grief doesn't just live in your heart—it lives in your body.

The emotional gravity of grief is undeniable even if your response is emotionless. What I didn't fully understand was how trauma doesn't just live in our minds—it settles physically. That's something Dr. Bruce Lipton explained beautifully to me: "When you experience an emotion, your brain releases chemistry into your blood, and that chemistry controls the fate of your cells."

Dr. Bruce Lipton, the author of *Biology of Belief*, appeared on my podcast because I was curious about the biological effects grief—or any profound emotional experience—can have on us. It always seemed obvious to me, even as a layperson, that grief doesn't just change us philosophically. It changes us *molecularly*.

The question becomes: *How long do we carry the emotional chemistry of our trauma?* Grief creates a physiological response—stress hormones and emotional chemicals flood our bloodstream. Left unaddressed, this can lead to chronic physical ailments. Trauma rewires brain function for survival, but at the cost of our body's ability to keep us healthy.

Thousands of years ago, humans faced immediate, life-threatening dangers—like sabertooth tigers. When one appeared, our bodies funneled all their energy into our arms and legs so we could fight or run. Stress hormones like cortisol and adrenaline surged, prioritizing survival over everything else.

But that biological response was meant for *immediate* survival, not prolonged exposure. Today, our "tigers" look different—they're our bills, our jobs, our grief. When stress becomes constant, it suppresses essential bodily functions and can even alter our genetic expression. Positive emotions, Dr. Lipton explained, can activate genes linked to healing. Negative emotions—like fear and prolonged grief—can activate genes associated with inflammation and disease.

In short: *stress kills us.*

I've heard many stories of people carrying prolonged emotional stress until it manifests as physical illness. And it's my top priority to reduce stress. Easier said than done. But I firmly believe we all have the capacity to minimize it, no matter what we're going through.

My larger point is this: our emotional health is inseparable from our physical health—they're two sides of the same coin. It reminds me of something author and hospital chaplain J. S. Park, who has witnessed thousands of deaths, told me: "Grief doesn't necessarily leave our body. We can suppress it, or we can name it."

When we suppress feelings, they don't just disappear—they settle into our bodies, sometimes showing up as physical illness, cognitive fog, or an unshakable exhaustion. J. S. Park emphasizes the variable of naming it. If we have the power to name our grief, we also hold the power to *define* it. A negative response to loss feels very natural. Imagine someone saying, "I have no reason to live after this death. They were taken from me and I'll never be happy again."

I've met very few people who decided to name their grief and pain in a transcendental "positive" way right in the beginning. I just see it as a temporary place we pass through and it's okay to have those thoughts because the pain is real. I just also believe we can reframe, name, and define these experiences. That's a heavy task, and often an unfair one to place on someone who's in the raw, swirling chaos of loss.

Imagine being in the eye of a hurricane, fighting just to stay upright, and someone leans in to tell you, "This is a lesson to live more presently and embrace everything you have." Yeah, thanks. Super helpful while trailer tractors are whizzing by my head.

Hindsight—when the winds have settled and the sky begins to clear—shows us something different. With intentional effort, and a little grace, we realize we have this almost *superhuman ability* to reframe sadness, to make sense of what feels senseless.

For me, those reframed perspectives led to a labyrinth of existential questions—ones I still explore when I can get my own head out of the way.

Grief in the Brain

Grief may not have a brain, but it certainly likes to pretend it does by hijacking our neurological pathways. Mary-Frances O'Connor, a clinical psychologist and author of *The Grieving Body,* introduced me to her work, emphasizing the biological and neurological impact of loss. The effect of grief can feel like a total eclipse of the heart. Light one moment, darkness in the next.

That darkness affects our entire biological and neurological imprint. Imprints that we often have a hard time even detecting are there. For the longest time I wondered how my brain chemistry was altered. I've learned that my brain may not only just be adjusting to this new world order, but it also has the incredible ability to trim the fat of information that may not be pertinent to us in the moment.

Mary-Frances explains, "It's not just emotional; your ability to focus, recall, and even make decisions can be impaired. The grieving brain is processing an enormous amount of change in the background."

I used to get frustrated at all the things I don't remember. I wanted to remember in more detail what I truly felt. What I was thinking. Banging my head against the metaphorical (and sometimes literal) wall becoming angry at myself for forgetting such pivotal moments of my life. But then my mother told me on our mother-son episode that *maybe I don't have to remember*. Maybe forgetting wasn't a biological failure as much as it was mercy.

Maybe not every memory is necessary. And this brain fog I've experienced most of my life was my body's way of protecting me. My brain was offering me neurological grace. I was more served by reflection rather than remembrance.

Mary-Frances said, "I have patients who tell me they don't remember months after a loss. Their brain wasn't just grieving—it was shutting down non-essential processes to protect them."

Looking at it this way is comforting. Yet, at the same time here it's a balancing act. Because she also explained that our brain can also treat grief suppression as a potential threat. And, that unacknowledged threat can curate negative biological expressions in the form of depression or anxiety.

To me, life is a process of constant recalibration. I feel different all the time, and I'm continually adjusting how I understand myself and the world around me. I think our brains are doing the same thing—always scanning for safety, always trying to protect us.

For a long time, I experienced that shift as something being wrong with me, as if my mind had become neurotic or broken. Now I see it differently. What I was actually grappling with was how to allow grief into my life—not as a problem to fix, but as something that now moves alongside me.

I can acknowledge that my brain has been rattled. And with the awareness of that, I become more attuned to what grief is capable of doing—to my thoughts, my memory, my nervous system. That awareness doesn't solve anything, but it gives me a way to live with it instead of fighting it.

We can give ourselves some grace merely by recognizing the intricate effect grief has not only on our hearts and our body but our brain. And, in that recognition we are more aware to pay attention to what has changed in us.

And once you realize grief affects your biology, it's hard not to start questioning everything—including the rest of stuff we can't see.

GRIEF IN THE SPIRIT

I was raised Catholic. The heaven-and-hell narrative wasn't force-fed at home, but Catholicism's structures—its rituals, doctrines, and the looming question of what happens after we die—were presented to me. But even as a kid, I was more of an *observer* than a believer. Also, I just didn't care.

But many years after losing my dad and others in my life—and then spending years talking about grief with people from every walk of life—I realized grief cracks you open. It didn't just make me ask, *Where did my dad go?* It eventually made me ask, *Where do any of us go?*

I've always leaned toward believing life continues in *some* form. The idea of nothingness never felt right to me, but I also can't fully dismiss the possibility. But then again, there's no way there isn't more than this.

There's magic all around us. I can just FaceTime my sister and see her 3,000 miles away through the ether and this invisible force of frequencies and I'm to believe it's impossible that we don't invisibly continue in some other form? Have you ever seen a platypus? That thing alone proves we have no idea what's really going on here.

Humor has always been my lifeline—it's the industrial tape holding together the cracked vase of my life. But filtered within the jokes is real curiosity. And over the years, that curiosity has led me to conversations with people across the entire belief spectrum.

Not in an overwhelming way, but in a way that showed me something important: **everyone is searching for meaning, even if they deny it.**

Take my mother. She had her own near-death experience in 2023. When I posted the conversation online, people in the comments called her a liar. My own mother. A liar. It was hilarious in its own way, but it also reminded me how uncomfortable people are with anything that challenges their worldview. Some people grow up believing their one perspective is the entire truth, so when someone else shares something different, they treat it as an attack instead of an invitation.

Not everyone wants or needs to explore. But I do.

Back to J. S. Park. He identified as an atheist until grief opened him up: "Sometimes I've seen so much where I'm like, 'God, what God?' And then there are other times where I'm like, 'I don't think I could do this without understanding that there is some sort of unchangeable source.'"

That push and pull—the emotional whiplash—is familiar to anyone who's buried someone they love. One day you feel connected to something bigger. The next day you're staring at the ceiling fan and spinning with it.

Claire-Bidwell Smith said something that stuck with me: "I feel like for the first time in my life, I've developed this thing called *faith*. And I don't even know what that means because it's not like on a Christian level or like anything like that. It's just like this weird faith and that there's something bigger than this."

It's not dogma. It's not doctrine. It's a quiet, internal shift.

And then, for balance, I talked to astrophysicist and writer Neil de Grasse Tyson. He explains death through the laws of physics, confirming the first law of thermodynamics that energy cannot be created or destroyed but just changed from one form to another. For him, this means we *do* continue—just not in the way we might imagine.

But then he says: "Personally, I don't have any reason to think that anything other than [my body decomposing] is going to happen to me. The energy contents of our body, itself reduced to ash, actually enter earth's atmosphere. It ultimately escapes to space in the form of infrared energy, radiating in all directions at the speed of light, filling the voids of the cosmos with her presence."

This exploration is exhilarating, terrifying, nonsensical, or exhausting depending on your perspective. But here's what I learned from all these different voices: people don't need the same explanation to arrive at the same truth or their own truth.

- A scientist might say we dissolve back into the universe without consciousness.
- A religious person might say we go home.
- A philosopher might say death is what gives life meaning.
- I might say we cross over, reconnect with those we love, learn something, and maybe even choose to come back.

Different roads. Same destination: **a making sense of the unknown.** And honestly, that's the beauty of it. The not knowing and customization of meaning.

We may never know. And yet, we keep asking, keep searching, keep hoping. Some seemingly don't search or care to ask these questions. If I'm being diplomatic then that's cool. But, if I'm being honest, then I think it's ill advised not to ask questions that enrich our lives with passionate exploration. The focus isn't just, "after we die." It's gripping on to what resonates with *you*.

We're still here in our meat suit bodies, trying to make sense of a world that can hurt deeply—and that's easier said than done.

Death has helped me explore this tug of war among faith, doubt, and curiosity.

Whether through science, faith, or philosophy, we can arrive at a similar place: gratitude. But the gravity of grief often drags us to the other end of the spectrum, where fear takes over.

All this searching eventually led me to one unavoidable truth: grief demands courage.

RUNNING TOWARD THE ROAR

In the animal kingdom, male lions could be seen as lazy while the lionesses do most of the hunting. But the male lion plays a crucial role. When prey gathers for water, the male lion roars from one side, causing the animals to panic and run the opposite direction—straight into the waiting jaws of the lionesses.

The lesson is simple:

Sometimes the safest place is the place you're running from.

Sometimes we have to take the chance and run *toward* the roar.

Grief works the same way. For a while, we run from the thing that terrifies us: our sadness, anger, the truth of what happened, or the truth of what we lost. Avoidance feels like protection. It feels instinctual. And sometimes no matter what direction we go we'll still get bit.

We can avoid the room they used to sit in, the song they loved, the photos they're in. We can avoid looking at the *footage*. We can bury ourselves in work, relationships, distractions, drinking, anything, or keep moving in the other direction.

The problem with pushing down grief is that it behaves like holding a beach ball underwater. The farther we push it down, the harder it rebounds and smacks us in the face.

But in the quiet. In the stillness. In the moments we least expect it, grief *will* resurface.

Because grief is meant to be felt. Faced. Expressed.

None of us gets to avoid the roar forever. The choice is ours: stay pinned under the weight of grief or use it as a foundation to build something meaningful. At your own pace. And that turning—however small and whenever you decide—is the beginning of healing. Never dramatic. Never the same as we were. More like a micro-shift. An exhale. A step, not a leap.

For me, facing the roar began with something unexpectedly simple: **letting myself feel, even when the feelings sucked.**

Because I think we need to feel the weight before we can build on it. To allow ourselves to be pulled down without resistance. Grief certainly can get worse before it gets better, because the truth is: when you finally turn toward it, it *will* get worse. You see all the things you've avoided. And that's painful as hell.

When I was about 18, I had terrible acne. This is a hard pivot, but stick with me. By the time I got to college, it was the worst it had ever been. I tried everything and finally ended up on Accutane, a last resort medication that basically nukes your face from the inside out. The dermatologist warned me, "It will get worse before it gets better."

I'd wake up every morning terrified to look in the mirror. Sometimes I kept the lights off just to avoid confirming what I already knew. I wore my hoodie low in class to hide the mountain of breakouts. I didn't have a brave moment of acceptance—I just got tired. Tired of hiding. Tired of avoiding what was.

So, I started looking.

Every day. Lights on. Face-to-face.

Carrying myself through the campus owning up to what everyone may see.

Then seeing myself got easier. Then it got a little better. Then a little better.

The roar got quieter.

Moving with grief works the same way.

You cannot fix what you refuse to look at.

You cannot outrun grief faster than grief can track you.

Sometimes it begins not with wisdom or courage but with finally being too tired to keep running. However long that may be for you. And that's okay.

Every step matters. Even the steps backwards. Every micro-moment of honesty. Every time you pause instead of sprinting the other direction. Even if you choose fear, that choice still teaches us something.

I just ask that you contemplate which direction you take your next move. There are no wrong feelings. This shit is scary. I just challenge you to challenge yourself. To hear the shots in the distance and run toward them. Because as counterintuitive as it may sound our salvation lies with the *perceived* danger. And often the danger isn't as dangerous as we imagine it to be.

Running from grief keeps us alive, but running toward it helps us live.

CHAPTER FOUR

THE POWER OF PERMISSION

"You're allowed to not be okay—and still want happiness."

—Michael Allio, Episode 236

My third-grade teacher at Nut Swamp Middle School was Mrs. Rosenthal. Whenever I would ask to go to the bathroom or request any sort of permission, I would phrase it as, "Can I go to the bathroom?" Mrs. Rosenthal would respond with a sassy tilted head and ask, "I don't know, can you?"

At eight years old, this was an existential crisis. Her rhetorical question made me wonder if I even knew how to use the bathroom anymore. My entire body tensed up as if she had asked me to explain the subtext of the Pythagorean theorem.

After a long pause and the fading ignorance of what a rhetorical question was, she would correct me: "*May* I go to the bathroom?"

This lesson stuck with me. Not just in etiquette, but in something much deeper: **the power of asking for permission.**

At the time, I thought this was a grammatical alteration, but looking back, Mrs. Rosenthal had unknowingly planted a seed—a seed that has sprouted into a fundamental truth about life, grief, and healing.

Often asking for permission is engrained in asking someone else for authorization to do something. In this context, it's asking yourself for permission. We spend so much of our lives asking for permission not only from others and society, but most surprisingly, from ourselves. And I'm not certain we even realize we're doing it.

On the surface, this should be an easy task because, after all, you're the director of your own actions, and you might even be an adult. We hesitate. We second-guess. We hold back joy, love, healing, and feeling—because somehow, we haven't self-authorized. What happens when we *don't* give ourselves permission to do something? What if we just decided to? Usually, there's a reason attached to it—a justification or explanation for why we shouldn't.

Pay attention to how your thoughts show up. They rarely arrive as statements. They come as questions. Unless the person next to you on the plane smells like holy hell and your brain clearly says, *She stinks,* most of our inner dialogue sounds like *Should I? Is this allowed? What if this makes things worse?*

I think both the "can I?" and "may I?" questions play a role when it comes to giving ourselves permission to feel and to find joy again after loss. Therefore, I'm declaring you deserve it, at a minimum. Permission to feel joy or to feel anything good is your birthright.

"Can I" asks about capacity. "May I" asks for permission. "I will" is an act of faith. The movement between them fluctuates, shaped by doubt and fear, until we're able—when we're ready—to step into "I will."

Often, grief began by questioning my capability, which then evolved to asking myself permission to feel a certain way, to finally stating that I will. And, then seven seconds later I'm doubting myself going backwards to questioning my ability or coming up with negative responses to why I shouldn't. A fluctuating wave that we can learn to surf.

That back-and-forth is okay. That's life. One moment I feel confident and the next moment, I don't. But as I mature, I'm learning to minimize those gaps and corrective responses to create a more positive outlook. An outlook that says I deserve to feel joy and I don't need to feel guilty about doing so.

Early in my life I'd ask, *Can I?* and the Google search engine of my brain would circulate all sorts of proposed answers that often leaned toward the negative what-ifs. I'd stay there for a long time. Now when I notice fear shaping my inner dialogue, I pause and flip my words on purpose, reinforcing the "I will" as a commitment rather than a question. Even when the doubt still feels present. Now when I pay attention to how I speak to myself I'll immediately fear and flip my words to train myself to say "I will" because I made the decision to continue forward. It always comes back to us. It comes back to our decision to choose and act. We give into thinking we have no ability to control our feelings. I believe we do. And, if you don't, I ask that you consider that *maybe* we do.

In grieving or in facing any of life's struggles, I've learned to give myself permission to feel and permission to find joy again—even in moments when my paradigms and current state of emotions tell me I shouldn't. Because it is okay to feel and it is okay to find joy.

I've listened to people who have lost their children, their husbands, their wives, their brothers in battle, siblings, cousins, grandparents, and have witnessed death in unimaginable ways. An undercurrent I've discovered in their stories is that they gave themselves the green light to feel—and to recognize that it is okay to find joy again. Alongside that, they gave themselves grace with the timing of it all. Even if it's just a moment of joy. There are no rules here.

It's the societal rules we see in movies, gossip, and even in stigmatized values about how we *should* grieve or feel. These cultural paradigms fog our minds with statements like "I can't believe they're dating already; it's only been 137 years since their spouse died."

I believe the inability to give yourself permission to find joy often stems from guilt. Well, I'm telling you it is okay to find joy. Even if you go right back to feeling like shit it is okay to look at a sunset and marinate in the beauty of the closing daylight. It's okay to laugh at a comedy you're watching on the TV because in this moment, even if it's brief, things are okay. Give yourself permission to experience those moments of joy. And, with intention and time you might just find yourself in a joyous life.

I have a deep faith in the perseverance and grit of the human spirit. And I've seen it over and over with the hundreds of stories I've been blessed to listen to.

As we begin to emerge from grief, it's common (even when it doesn't feel common) to feel resistance. Not just to the pain, but to the moments of relief. Joy can feel confusing, even threatening, as if allowing it means leaving something or someone behind. And, once we start to give ourselves permission to it, all these barriers can start to yield.

Acknowledge your feelings: Examine what you're feeling. Examine it with a lens of it being a feeling. Without attaching a storyline to it, just see it as what it is. A feeling. *What is it you feel?*

Challenge the inner critic: When your mind tells you it's "too soon" to feel joy, ask yourself, *Where does this come from? Did you read this? Hear this?*

Celebrate small wins: Did you smile today? Did you enjoy one small moment without guilt? Did you laugh at yourself for doing something incoherently stupid today?

Write yourself a permission slip: Literally. Write down "I give myself permission to feel joy, to grieve in my own way, and to live fully again." Sign it. Just don't ask for Mrs. Rosenthal's signature.

Practice self-compassion: Talk to yourself like you might talk to a friend in need.

Practice self-compassion (Aggressive Version): Talk to yourself like you're sick of living like this and you're going to change your ways and take the bull by the horns!

Compassion. You don't always have to be so hard on your damn self. Sometimes we have to just get ourselves off our ass. After the rephrasing of these questions to more of a definitive statement, you've now become your own Mrs. Rosenthal, authorizing your emotional bathroom pass.

Start with a light, respectful way of telling yourself with grace that you're allowed to find joy again. Truly dive into these philosophical semantics. Deeply examine where your mind races, which more often than not is negative. What are the reasons you're conjuring up that tell you not to find joy, not to feel? These are answers you need to address for a life unexamined is life not worth living.

Until we can give ourselves permission to live our life, to find joy, to feel, then we're just stuck. People get offended when I say this but if you want to stay stuck, then go ahead. But, at some point we need to be accountable for our own life separate from external events.

PERMISSION IN THE INTENSIVE CARE UNIT (ICU)

On July 13, 2023, I had a flight booked to Europe from Los Angeles to take a solo adventure.

Side note: planes apparently are a consistent traumatic theme in my life.

The morning of my flight was messy. I was a few months out of a relationship, and my ex was the one driving me to the airport. Now looking back, a $50 Uber and an unsolicited political conversation with an Uber driver would probably have been a wiser decision but so it goes.

Our goodbye wasn't amicable. The weight of guilt, emotional discomfort, yet relief weighed heavily on me as I rushed to the wrong terminal. Nevertheless, I made my flight.

As I walked onto the plane I was doing my mental gymnastics and breath work to let go of the moment that passed and find peace in the exciting adventure I was about to embark on. Every time I sit down I make it a point to say hello to the person I'm assigned to sit next to. Some may find that annoying but in my book a little acknowledgment that we'll be 3 inches from one another for 10 hours deserves a greeting. I didn't get a response and at first thought this dude was a bit of a dick but, hey, you never know what someone is going through.

Boy, was I wrong.

Despite not checking in the emotional baggage at the gate, I found myself next to an actor from one of my favorite movies. We spent hours talking, laughing, and drinking. It was exactly what I needed.

After about eight hours of banter and quite a lively buzz, the plane was descending for a final crescendo. I made it to Europe with a rejuvenated heart and vitality. Until it wasn't.

The budget airline I was flying on didn't have Wi-Fi. And, as the plane taxied I turned on my phone to connect and saw messages from both my sisters. It was another moment etched in time that would reshape my life. "David, call us please if you get this."

It was one of those moments where you know it's not going to be good. I knew before I even called back that this was eerily similar to the walk around the bend that something bad had happened. My sister Gina never messaged me on WhatsApp. It was completely irregular. It was one of those moments when the energy drained from my body in anticipation of what could come.

Still on the plane, I call my eldest sister Jacqueline immediately who calmly and directly tells me, "Mom went into cardiac arrest. Her heart stopped. She made it to the hospital. You have to come home."

I leaned forward toward the seat in front of me digesting the many particles of thought racing through my head. An odd calm rushes over my body as my elbow stabilizes my hand on my forehead before I respond to my sister. It felt like my body wanted to go out of body but checked itself before it left me. I collected myself and told her I'm coming.

My flight buddy sitting next to me noticed how distraught I was. He asked if I was okay and I said to him that I have to get to Jersey, my mom's heart stopped. He exhaled understanding that words weren't necessary.

I was in processing mode. I don't want to call it shock despite it being shocking. It oddly felt like a controlled shock but nevertheless I was putting fragments of myself back together that slowly felt as if I was breaking into a billion pieces into the ether. I thought to myself staring into the fabric of an airline passenger seat, "There's no way. This isn't how it happens. This isn't it. There's no way."

I felt with passion that this isn't how my mother dies. This isn't how the story goes. But, then my brain kicks into another gear to squabble up with my emotions saying, *This could be it. This very well could be how she goes.* After balancing the scales and understanding I played enough of this game it was time for motion.

My new friend helped me find guest services to find a flight back to the States. We exchanged numbers and that man continued to check in with me as time passed. My trip ended before it even started and that was the least of my concerns.

The quickest flight I could get was several hours away so I had time to pass. From Gatwick Airport I hopped on the train to my hotel, which was over an hour or so away. I scrambled to my hotel to charge my phone in the lobby notifying the front desk I would not be staying. Time stood still. The illusion of time couldn't move fast enough to get back on a plane back to Jersey.

My brother-in-law Jeff called me to check in, offering me natural comfort just to hear his voice. Even as I type this I feel the emotion and synchronicities like a repeat of history when Jeff was here again keeping me steady just like the following weeks of 9/11 playing video games with me.

I realized in the moments of waiting the similarities to the day my dad died.

Instead of being in school with no contact with my family, I was on a plane with no Wi-Fi. Instead of waiting for David to come home from school, it was waiting for David to get off his flight and come home. Again, it was my family waiting for me after me. Only this time I'm a grown man peculiarly feeling prepared for this moment.

These thoughts were downloaded into my head in a split second as I went to the nearest bar to sit by myself and sip on something strong.

With constant updates from my family while I was isolated thousands of miles away across the cold Atlantic I prevented myself from the what-if Google search engine questions in my mind. I still held firmly this wasn't how my mother went but couldn't escape the thought that she could be dead before I even get on my flight back. Either way, I knew what was in my control and what wasn't. All I could do was allow myself to naturally react and choose my response. Freaking out and succumbing to the clear possibility my mother may be gone doesn't serve my mother, my family, or myself in this moment. Even though it felt like a time for fight or flight (literal flight in this case) it felt odd. It felt as if another mode kicked in when I was reminded of this tool belt that I had based on past experience and all that I've gathered from my work. With this tool belt I wasn't immune to the gravity of emotions, uncertainty, and being human. But, something felt familiar with a knowingness that all will be okay even when it's not. It was bizarre.

The time came to take another train ride from London to Heathrow and get on another flight back to Jersey.

It felt me versus me on that flight back. My mind was in a tortoise versus the hare race to the finish line of Newark Airport. The hare of my thoughts were the favorite moving at a rapid almost dangerous place of imagination of what would happen. But, I attempted to find solace in the slow pace of the tortoise to slow everything down. There's only so much in my control. While on this seven-plus-hour return flight I had thoughts that made me realize how eerily similar this was to that day 22 years ago on September 11. Instead of being in school away from my family wondering about David, I was on a plane across the pond.

This isn't where I tie in the theme of permission just yet. Fuck permission right now. This is fight or flight. This is a time where permission can take a back seat in economy and I do whatever it takes. Permission usually comes later post-grief . . . so I thought.

I land in Newark. Thankfully my ex wasn't waiting there for a ride and I learned my lesson to call an Uber for another hour or so commute.

I make it to my mother's building where my beautiful sister waited for my arrival outside. It's now 1:00 a.m. My sister persuaded the nurses to allow me into the ICU past curfew to see my mother on a breathing tube.

Arguably the most raw, visceral feeling that I'll never forget. This could be it. But, it can't be, my mind seesawed.

As if grappling with this reality wasn't enough the nurse notified my sister and me that my mother had herself down as a DNR. Do not resuscitate.

Jesus, Mary, and Joseph . . . what, mom?!?

No need to go into the hard details of that process to override that decision but it points out the multiple facets of these types of experiences—the details that come outside of the obvious concern during heavy moments in life.

To get you to the climax of this story, my mom is alive, despite the doctors having no explanation. Before she got out of the hospital the doctor literally told us to go to Vegas because it's a miracle that she's not only alive but also that there's no long-term damage; she's in incredible shape. That week would be filled with a roller coaster ride and a script that Quentin Tarantino couldn't write. The stories within that week, the emotions, the ups, the downs, the pain, the beauty, the familial connection have changed my life.

It's the full-circle oddity of permission that came in for me at the most unexpected moment. This is a phase that I thought came later down the road when I finally allowed myself to feel, find joy, yada yada yada.

Notice how this "grief advice" comes in the form of *yada yada yada* when you're in it. I'll never forget how present I felt in the ICU during the most precious uncertain and heaviest time. The presence I felt in the hospital room not knowing if my mother would survive. And, if she did survive, would she be a vegetable? Will her memory or motor functions of a woman so in shape and athletic ever be the same?

As she improved as we slowly learned that she was going to be okay.

It's the almost eerie feeling of presence I felt. Something on the spot I gave myself permission for. I allowed myself to feel everything. I allowed myself to laugh with my family with my mom's near lifeless body next to us because I know not only is that okay (with my sick dark sense of humor) but it's also what she would want.

I gave myself permission in the moment of impossible certainty to feel everything I was feeling without hindrance. To be here.

I gave myself permission dare I say feel joy while I'm sitting next to my mother's potential deathbed. It sounds sadistic but to me it was beautiful. My family and I still found brief moments of levity beside her. I know that you can find joy in the most dire of moments even if the joy is for a moment because I lived it.

Again, this. A unique situation because the permission usually comes later. It comes maybe days, months, years down the road with grief and in this case anticipatory grief.

But, in this cluster shit of a live event, it was as if my family and I were prepared for this. The way we were able to glide through living and grieving, living and feeling, feeling pain and still finding joy, and the beauty in the way my sisters and family mellifluously operated during desperate times was permission to me.

Of course, I thought I shouldn't laugh during this time, I shouldn't feel the proudness of witnessing the strength of my sisters during this time because this was fight or flight. I should feel anticipatory grief, sadness, pain, worry, and all the negative shit only!

I don't buy into that.

This was a lesson that even through the most difficult times there is still joy to be found but it won't be found until we give ourselves the permission. And, this processing for me was happening in real time. With my father, it took years of contemplation to recognize the power of permission and grace. But, for whatever reason I felt I had the tools in our tool belt to leverage this thing called permission even in the moment.

You give me an actual Phillips head screwdriver and I'll stab my hand somehow. But, this set of tools was psychosomatic and spiritual.

In the ICU, I wasn't just asking *Can I feel joy right now?* but rather *May I?* and finally saying *I can* and *I will*. In my own style alongside the people I love most.

As I sat beside my mother, I realized this was a "may I?" moment. The weight of the permission wasn't on ability—it was on grace. Mrs. Rosenthal, you sneaky sassy woman who gave me no recess for a full week after vandalizing the bathroom, you prepared me for this moment all along. This lesson flipped into something more profound than etiquette—it taught me about owning *my* internal narrative and granting myself the grace in doing so.

Permission isn't a one-time thing. It's a daily whisper, a quiet allowance, a breath you take. And it starts with asking yourself—not Mrs. Rosenthal—*May I?*

This self-granted permission opens up a whole new world to experience life and enables us to define our experiences rather than let the experience define us.

And, it's ironic how full circle this event was not only in the comparison of the similarities of me being away from my family in school or in this case across the ocean. I had this painful experience with my family as a man instead of a boy. A boy who was the man of the house now. A boy who carried the weight of guilt uncertain if I ever was enough of a support system for my mother, sisters, and family.

This experience enabled me to grasp the situation with a more developed mind and heart. I was finally ready to be that support system even though if you ask my mom I already was. I carried that guilt for so long and this was my moment to be there for my family as much as they have always been there for me. My sisters were incredible during this time, as they've been my entire life. I am in awe of them.

For me personally it was my time to step up and be the rock for my sisters the best I can. I wasn't perfect. No one is. But, I was finally able to instinctively be there and feel as if I could close that chapter of guilt. That wasn't the selfish driving force. It's in my nature but when the dust settled I made this realization. And, it was my sister Jacqueline who said to me that she didn't see me as her little brother anymore in how I was able to be there for them. A validation I didn't ask for. She just told me. It was that moment in her kitchen my eyes watered, as if they were words the 12-year-old boy in me needed to hear.

Life has a funny way of prepping us for the rest of life. There are hidden lessons that don't show up in our head until we need it. Without the experiences our family had in the past I'm not sure we would have been able to navigate the near-death of my mother as we did. We gave ourselves permission, whether we realized it or not, to feel it all and go through this experience.

I know my mother wouldn't want us in that hospital without grace, levity, and compassion, not only for her but for her children. Even if she died on that hospital bed. I have no right to say what your loved one would think or want, but I want you to answer for yourself if your loved one would want you stuck—and if they would want you to find joy again.

Give yourself that permission.

CHAPTER FIVE

LOSS AS A GAIN

"You're not just missing them—you're missing what was supposed to happen."

—Gary Sinise, Episode 218

Every night, five days a week, I'd hear the garage door open like the sound of muffled thunder in the distance. It was a positive trigger to sprint to the garage door from wherever I was. It meant my father was home from work.

It was like the adrenaline rush of a roller coaster at Six Flags—charged with unconditional love. Sometimes I'd time it so well that when I got to the garage door, he'd just be opening it.

Whether my dad was having a great day or a difficult day I was completely ignorant as I'd rush in for a hug obliterated with excitement that my father is home. I can still feel the fabric of his suit against my cheek. I felt safe and loved unconditionally.

Now when I hear garage doors open it takes me back to these memories. At the time, I was completely oblivious that I'd grow into a man, move out of the house, and not have these moments. But when he died, I hadn't grown up yet. Those moments were ripped away too soon. Every night, I grieved this one simple routine.

But grief doesn't just take one thing from you—it takes *many*.

The death of someone starts with a macro-loss and cascades into a seemingly infinite list of micro-losses that often reveal themselves over time.

It's losing the call you'd get every afternoon.

It's sleeping alone for the first time in 30 years.

It's the friend you'd send texts to without second-guessing just to share a new accomplishment.

It's the way your person knew how much salt to put in your scrambled eggs—a loss you may not realize until two months later the next time a waiter asks you how you like your eggs.

It's a waterfall of micro-losses that aren't to be ignored or minimized. Because when you consolidate these little details they add up to a whole *life*. When things are quiet and you're moving with the initial chaos of hanging on for dear life. The micro-losses are often losses we don't recognize until we're in the exact moment of that which we lost. And the realization can be shocking.

I wasn't thinking about my baseball games in the immediate days after my dad's death. But, that first game back when I was on the mound was one of those moments. I'd glance into the bleachers waiting and eventually seeing that my dad made the game straight from work. Then the time came for me to habitually look into the crowd only to remember my dad won't be making this game.

It's like being in the passenger seat of a car daydreaming and then whoever is driving slams on the breaks. An "oh, shit" moment I wasn't even aware I lost until I was in it. A reopening of just one jigsaw piece to work through. A micro-loss among the macro-losses.

It's the little pieces of life that went slightly unnoticed—until they were gone.

Death is a funny thing. It takes someone from you but often leaves an invisible guiding hand if you allow it. Because what's left is a whole slew of routines, habits, and shared experiences that have become engrained in our life.

And what I've learned is not to wait for *it* to be gone to realize what you have. There's not a better way to learn than through experience but learning from others' experiences can be pretty damn good if you allow it to register.

The sneaky part of grief—the *after*. After the funeral. After the flowers. After the lasagna stops showing up at your doorstep. When the noise quiets down and you realize the world around you is still part of the regularly scheduled programming. And you're left with the silence.

And in that silence, it gets louder. You start to realize that grief isn't just about *who* you lost. It's about *how* your entire life changes in their absence. There is a compounding effect of realizing what life was to and contrasting that to what life is now.

It feels like walking into a different dimension—one you didn't choose, but now have to manage living in. It can be rearranging daily routines that constantly remind us of our loss. This is why people call it a *new normal*. What was once normal has been completely shattered into a new way of living. The oxymoron of death is this: it's the most normal thing in the world, yet everything it leaves behind feels anything but.

It's an adjustment to a new life. A life with different routines and habits to create. Remembering the micro-losses for a long time made me sad. And sometimes it still does. But in a different way. It's morphed into a realization that I got to have those moments. And I feel grateful for being able to pull back these feelings as if they're actively happening.

And now it's gratefulness.

The '96 Ford Bronco I bought in my father's memory has shown me the alchemy of grief. Pain to gratitude. Whenever I'd see a White Ford Bronco I'd feel a throb in my chest that now has morphed into a little smirk.

That smirk represents my entire journey of pain transformed into thankfulness. A representation of what once sparked sadness converted to being grateful that I get to still *feel* my father. I like thinking about my dad. It just took time to adjust to this completely new relationship.

It took going through it. It took processing. It took time. At the end of the day my perspective on the many forms of losses are a reminder to notice all the things I can potentially lose.

That potentiality of loss makes me savor everything in my life now. Not in the form of fear or latching on to suffocation but to hold everything gently. With the gentle grasp comes an appreciation that allows room for it to slip from my hand at a moment's notice.

I used to get so frustrated when I'd meet people who complained about their parents. I'd be mentally grinding my teeth screaming inside "at least you still have your dad!" I'd take the natural perspective that I only had my father for 12 years. I lost the last two-plus decades of having a father.

Now I don't think like this. I feel so blessed to have had 12 years with my father. Instead of decades lost, it's 12 years gained. My father made a short pit stop on this earth and I was blessed enough to be part of it while it was here. This may be a tough pill to swallow for most, but I didn't lose, I gained.

There's wisdom in knowing of that which we will lose is something we've gained.

A prior guest, Laura Shepard, spoke of her dad and taught me the perspective of seeing a loss as a gain.

> Right after he passed away, I was thinking a lot about it, and I was thinking I want to see it not so much as a loss, but rather as a life that I gained or experienced for a time. So, for a time my dad and my path intersected in the universe, and I got to know him, and he got to know me, and that's something that I gained, something that I had. And then now like I've moved on to another chapter I like to see it that way and I think just viewing life and death that way is just really helped me be more present and not so afraid of dying.

And, not so afraid of not having. We don't really *have* anything. We just get to experience it for a while.

What stays, stays.

What goes, goes.

Ultimately, this practice has made me more present. Instead of focusing on how a moment will inevitably end, it keeps me in the pocket of seeing it as a moment I just gained. I get to sit here with my mother while I'm visiting New Jersey knowing the time will come where I have to leave. And, when the time comes to leave, I know I appreciated the moment when it was exactly that, a moment.

Of course, I want more time with my mother. As an inherent glutinous human, I always want more of the good stuff. When I find myself wanting more it takes me out of what's right in front of me. What is here right now. A moment, an experience or a person that I gained in this life. Even though I know it won't be here forever. When I see this all as a gain, then I never really lost.

As if managing the river of emotions wasn't enough already, we have to mourn the person we were when they were alive. It's about managing the way we see things because it takes energy. That simple perspective shift (which is anything but simple) can make a huge difference in how we move through life after loss.

But the micro-losses don't just live in routines or rituals. They seep into who we are. Because when the people we love disappear, parts of us do, too.

IDENTITY LOSS 2.0

You're a father. You're a wife. A son. A daughter. A friend.

All these often self-curated titles. After loss it can feel like we shed these titles moving forward. You no longer feel like yourself anymore because we had a purpose tied to that someone. If you lose your kid, are you still a father? If you are a widow, are you still a wife? If you lose your parents, are you still a daughter?

Titles can be a big part of our identity. Then we feel we have to rewrite our title. To others it seemed I was no longer a son, but the boy who lost his dad on September 11.

This new title affected me. I felt that I made the baseball team because of what happened to me. I was good but I don't think I had any business making the team as a 7th grader. I recognized this even then. Whether that is true or not I was aware of a difference in the way I was treated. Because I now had a new identity to *others* not only to myself. There comes the need for some sense of accountability to allow others' perceptions to affect me or not.

At this point of my life I don't care how others perceive me because no one knows most of the details of my experience. But the way we are perceived can certainly have an impact on the identity we give ourselves. It's up to us to decide to accept that identity or to create our own.

Who we want to be isn't exactly in the forefront of most people's minds amid grief. We're just trying to survive. It's more about being aware.

Often, this awareness creates some organization, even if we need to step away from it and return later. You don't have to know who the new you will be, just that there will be one. And, who says you need to pigeon-hole yourself into just one identity?

PERSPECTIVE OVER PRESCRIPTION

There is no one prescription to cure us. Ultimately, it comes down to how we perceive everything.

I was a son to my father. Now I'm not. That's the logical progression.

But, to me nothing feels logical about the grief experience. My perspective often feels illogical. Of course, I'm not a son to my father anymore. He's dead.

Then I sit in that and think, no, I am forever the son to my father. Whether he is here or not. As the son to my father, it is the inherited duty to look after my mother, my sisters, and the fruit to bear. My role as a son remains. Not in the physical relationship with my father directly but still a lot of the same duties.

I have a choice to look at not being a son to my father anymore or step up even more in my role now that he's gone. My mother lost her husband and her direct role as being a wife that won't ever truly be replaced, but she's forever my father's wife. We don't have to remove the title because the logistics have changed.

Can you straw argument this theory I'm proposing? Sure. But I choose to keep it simple. A simple mindset that to me offers comfort. I am still my father's son. My dear friend Veronica, who died too soon in her twenties, is still my friend. My grandparents are still my grandparents. These slight variations in wording offer me more comfort. It keeps what's not alive still alive.

It's not avoiding acceptance; it's a small variation of perceiving these identities that we lost, curated, created: it's a recreation if anything.

It's keeping some sense of normalcy through the most abnormal (yet most normal since we're all going to die) of times.

Maybe the prescription is in the perspective. As silly and small as these shifts may seem, they've changed the way I move through grief and life. The absurd part is identity is only a fraction of all we have to manage during this process. The identity is something we deal with presently every day but what about the moments that we know won't come?

The moments we know will never come are in the future. And this has been the most challenging part for me.

LOSS OF FUTURE

The thing about plans is that they rarely go to plan.

For anyone that has dealt with death will understand this notion. Sure, there may be exceptions for the beautiful souls who lived way beyond receiving social security. But when we lose a loved one too soon the micro-losses we face are also in the plans.

The future that never showed its face.

Some of the growing pains of my experience was the realization I never got to have my first legal beer with my father. I won't be able to have the man-to-man talks where I can hear the not-so-good parts of my dad. The stories that a father can only tell his son when he reaches a certain age.

My entire future with my father vanished before it could ever have the chance to exist. So, one day I find peace in that my father is gone and then I'm having a beer with my friend and his father and it feels like I've just been in a mental car accident. The weight of realizing I won't have this is heavy. It's a void that I feel will never be filled. An entire future of experiences and potential memories stopped in its tracks.

You had plans of having children. Of growing old together. Plans to take that golf trip with your boys when the kids are old enough. We have it in our minds that we have time and that this is supposed to be until we're old and gray. That's just not the way it works. Plans are only plans until they don't go as planned.

And here we are again to make a choice. A choice that might not seem like a choice. I didn't ask for this experience. But we have a choice to work with the power of how we perceive things. When I'm at the bar with my best friend's father who is like another father to me, I still get a feeling of what it's like to have a father. He won't ever be my father. He won't ever replace my father. But I feel a piece of my father in these moments. I get to have the man-to-man conversations with a father figure. A different experience that I would trade for 1,000 lifetimes to have my father back, but I can't. So, while I'm here navigating and managing this grief journey, I will choose to make the best of it and find the micro-moments that can shift the macro.

Nothing will replace those lost. And it's not about replacing. It's about moving things around.

The love we got to have can be moved around. When they say grief is love with nowhere to go; I don't agree. The love still exists. Love is beyond the physical. We can move that love around to still love those who are gone but extrapolate it to our relationships and the relationship with the world.

I still hear that garage door sometimes—the same muffled thunder of his return. Only now, I don't sprint toward it. I just listen. Because it reminds me that I had something worth running toward. And losing what was worth running toward has taught me where life's real gold is found.

CHAPTER SIX

WHERE THE GOLD IS

"We don't grow from trauma. We grow from how we respond to trauma."

—David Kessler, Episode 145

As I've mentioned, I was raised Catholic and live as if nothing is absolute. But every now and then I attend a Bible study in which one of my best friend's father, Warren, flies in from Dallas to talk to a small group of us. I adore the way he speaks in analogies and stories sewn with lessons that stem from the Bible but reverberate into themes of navigating life.

He told me a tale of when he was a child and played marbles with his friends. One day, it was about to get dark but they hadn't finished their game. Withstanding the itch to continue their game and make it home before dark they decided to leave the game exactly as it was on the ground to revisit the next day. But that night came a thunderstorm sure to rumble the earth that held their marbles in place. On returning to the game, they discovered their marbles buried and engulfed in mud, barely recognizable. What once was shiny was now filthy.

Instead of stomping his feet in frustration he picked each one up and wiped the mud off until the mud revealed the marbles' original shine. Warren said to us, "The storms of life come in many different forms." And, that the storms *will* come. Storms can rock us to our core and yet there are foundations within us that are completely unshakable. When our metaphorical marbles get buried in the mud we can still uncover the beauty that was always there.

That's where the gold is.

It's the difficult times that muddy our marbles. In times where the darkness covers the light. Let's not forget the key word in that is *covered*. The light is not gone. The beauty of life's marbles just needs to be wiped off. Or we can leave them dirty.

Of all life's great lessons that have thrust me into being who I am today, it's always come from times of uncertainty, difficulty, and discomfort. When we choose to look at these obstacles and the new "normal" as a reminder as to what is important, then you've struck gold. It's not about when you find it, or how you find it. Searching for lessons in pain can feel forced and sometimes seemingly pointless. Revelation, when it comes, tends to arrive naturally. And this isn't about justifying the storm as some necessary or worthy sacrifice.

It's just about recognizing that the beauty isn't gone. It's just covered in mud. Mud that, sometimes, is easy to wipe off while other times it gets dry and crusty because we left it there and that needs a deeper cleanse.

WHERE THE GOLD WASN'T OBVIOUS

Fallon Farrinaci grew up in a small Métis community in Canada, living life that she intently expressed was a normal life with her parents and two brothers. In 1992, a local man became obsessed with her mother, stalking and threatening her. Law enforcement failed to act, dismissing multiple reports of threats when her mother explicitly warned them.

On January 27, 1993, he invaded their home, held Fallon's older brother hostage, and then murdered both of her parents before killing himself. Fallon was only nine years old. As she grew older, Fallon faced additional losses to add to the layers of the trauma she's persevered through—her older brother died by suicide at 29, and later, her younger brother also took his own life.

Even decades later, as one would expect, her eyes swell up with tears as she runs me through intense details of her experience. Within the gaps of words where she would collect herself I was digesting everything she was telling me. The silence between thoughts was paralyzing as she viscerally brought me back in time through this harrowing event. As I listened to this painful story I couldn't help but get teary-eyed myself.

However, throughout the conversation she expressed gratefulness and a sense of compassion despite having gone through events that defy reason.

Even as I write a chapter about how the trauma of life reveals the beauty at the same time I started to doubt myself on how the violent situation she endured could ever produce something like a lesson. So, I asked her how she's endured the years and was there anything positive she could conjure up from what she's been through.

Through immense grief, Fallon recognized the power of community and the support she had around her and how that helped her get through it. And, how that community not only carried her through but also presented a light in humanity when she had been a first-hand witness to an evil that could overtake her.

"I remember the night after it happened—my aunts and uncles were just there. They didn't have to say anything. They were just there . . . I was lying on my couch, completely devastated. And my friends were just there. They didn't try to fix it. They just sat with me." She didn't find community; community found her and therefore it was revealed to her.

She had all this support around her, and understood that not everyone has that. After going through one of the most horrendous things a human can experience at the young age of nine, it's incredible she doesn't harbor a complete disdain for humanity and existence.

Fallon learned the power of people coming together, and knew that kept her alive. She also saw how the actions of others in life and during times of turmoil gives meaning. And, through this recognition of community she continued that notion into building a community of her own from the impacts of her own experience.

Her family is of Indigenous backgrounds, and she educated me on the dark statistics of murdered and missing Indigenous women and girls affected by systematic failures in law enforcement. She's since used her story to bring change, raise funds for Indigenous organizations, and inspire others to find healing through community and purpose. "I don't believe that 'everything happens for a reason.' But I do believe that if I'm still here, I have to make it mean something."

We shared a brief exchange understanding that she would swap that day without thought for any teachings that she pulled from this. But she can't. So, while she's still here she decided to transmute her pain into purpose. And, though it had to come with grace it came also with a mindset of grit to not allow her experience to define her. We can't control what happens to us, but we control what we make of it.

I've listened to stories of people that have gone through horrid things. Things that I don't always have the experiences to empathize with but can sympathize with. Depths of darkness and sludge that on paper it sometimes doesn't make sense how someone can still have a smile on their face. But they do.

Time and time again I've seen so many amazing, kind, compassionate, and happy people once drenched in mud now walking in clean linens. It's a reminder that it can be done. And, when we're so deep that we don't see any possibility of light we can lean into other people's stories to give us hope.

Even though I often contemplate the mantra that someone *always has it worse,* I reflect on the turmoil in my life. I am proud of how I look at life. There are very few things that are better than walking out of the other side of the fire. Sure, I have some scars that may not be visible. But those scars are just a reminder of the pain and the sorrow that I've endured. And, with those scars that is where I've discovered the beautiful, shiny gold of life.

It's understanding the roller coaster of life that we are on. Challenges have come and will come. Perhaps my mother instilled this duality with equal parts toughness and softness. The grit of *not today*. This will not break me. I will beat this. A sense of accountability that I have control in how I move through life regardless of what lands in my way.

A competitive fire within me that I have to want to overcome. Blended with softness to keep my edge from becoming a chip on my shoulder. I keep the door ajar believing that somehow that whatever pain I may endure today will be used tomorrow. And, if not tomorrow then someday.

I don't simply believe life happens *to* us. And while I choose to believe it happens *for* us, I am okay with just letting things happen.

LIFE IS JUST HAPPENINGS

"By not striving, all things happen naturally."

—Chapter 48, *Tao Te Ching*

Chinese philosopher Laozi warns against excessive effort and romanticizing of control. By trying to force outcomes we disrupt the natural process, whereas a step back allows events to unfold organically. This doesn't mean passivity but rather acting in alignment with the natural process.

To me that natural process can seem chaotic. As if we're floating in air grasping at anything to hold on to. And it feels unnatural because it takes us out of whatever baseline state that has felt "natural" to us.

The *Tao Te Ching* discusses happening not as an action to us but as it being just that. A happening. The concept of *wu wei,* effortless action or non-interference. The best way to let things happen is to flow with it. Like being guided by the rip current.

I've been taught that if I were ever caught in a riptide of the ocean to not to swim against it, and almost not to swim at all. To let the tide take you because when you don't fight it you'll naturally be able to swim out without resistance. The challenge is knowing when the riptide has you and staying calm—it's such a terrifying shock to the system that our natural reaction is to freak out.

With this concept it relieves the pressure of trying to figure out what to do next. Trusting the happenings of life will naturally guide us out to safety. A trust in ourselves that we will know what to do even when we don't. Despite the innate panic we can find our center. We don't have to have actionable steps right away but we can flow with what it is we're going through and trust that the steps will follow.

Gold miners don't wander randomly. They follow old stories, history, mineral strains, river bends, and places others have found gold before. They dig and most of the time find nothing. The process is monotonous.

They use several tactics on repeat: dig, haul, and repeat. Then a miner might catch a hint—an inspiration in the form of a flake or a small speck. They haven't hit the jackpot, but there's evidence. A signal to keep going.

When enough flakes begin to appear, the miner doubles down and moves to the next level of tools. This is when the separation begins. Gold is heavy; debris washes away. A miner swirls water, letting the dirt wither away as the gold sinks. At this point, the miner doesn't have gold in its true form. What remains is still mixed with rock and sediment—ready for refining.

Gold is refined by fire. Extreme heat melts it down to only what's essential. Though most of the dirt is gone, it remains imperfect. As the gold liquifies, it loses its shape and impurities rise to the surface. The fire doesn't destroy the gold, it reveals what isn't gold.

The molten gold is then poured into molds, cooled, and given a new shape. The first time it truly looks like gold.

Once refined, gold has many uses. It can become currency, tools, jewelry, or mementos. Once the gold is found, it's up to the next person to decide what's done with it.

Just like the gold miner, after loss we begin to pay attention. It's not completely random. We notice memories, emotions, conversations, and questions. We don't know exactly what we're looking for or when we'll find it, but something tells us it matters.

Even when we do it again and again, we often find nothing. Just mud. It's not about the way we dig as much as it is about perseverance. We can try therapy, read books, listen to podcasts, scream into our pillows, and still feel like nothing is working—only accumulating more mud.

It becomes monotonous. We wake up, get through the day, repeat the same efforts, and feel no progress. Growth in grief hides in the repetition of perseverance. Even when not apparent.

Like the miner who finds a single flake, we may catch a moment of peace—a day that doesn't feel so crushing. It's not completion, just evidence. Enough to keep going.

Gold is heavy and so is grief. Loss forces us to audit everything—our beliefs, expectations, plans, and identity. Trivial priorities wash away like dirt, leaving only the essentials.

Even then, the work isn't done. What remains is still messy before it's useful.

This is where the fire comes in. The intense heat of grief and pain reshapes the rest of our lives. It's not the burning we endure but what comes after—the gold.

Finding gold in grief isn't about luck. It's about staying in the process long enough to melt down to our purest form. The pain is in the digging. Confusion is the dirt, repetition and showing up is the work. Evidence appears in small specks, not chunks of gold without a timeline.

Grief isn't a transformation, it's mining. You dig when you don't want to. You keep going when you don't see results. And then one day, you find a flake. Then another. Then another.

Those small specks keep us going, because grief doesn't hand us gold on a silver platter. It buries it. It offers us a chance to uncover it through effort and endurance.

And once we find the gold, our new life begins. What we do with it in its new form is up to us.

We don't have to wait for tragedy to be grateful and to find the gold.

WHEN IT HAPPENS TO YOU

Having lost my father in the way I did, I always reflect on the realization of, *Oh, shit, this really can happen to me*. It isn't just a news headline that I'm detached from and can passively say "Oh, those poor people." It's almost like a tragic comedy, this life of ours. The funny part isn't the tragedy, though I often will find the humor in it. Life is absurd in that eventually it shits on everyone.

Without the difficult parts of my life, I wouldn't see people the way I see them. My gold is that my experiences have made me more patient, to take things less personally and to understand the difference between the things I can change and the things I cannot. My love for others has only grown.

To be clear this wasn't a flip of the switch—this took time. And, we have to give it time. We need time to let the universe reveal the outcome even if we're terrified that how we feel now is how we'll feel forever.

And in that waiting, uncertainty clouds our decisions.

Grief is uncertain. Grief rattles our world, reality, mind, body, and soul so much that we often can't see one step in front of us. We don't know how we're going to continue. We don't know how we're going to be able to live or if this feeling is ever going to dwindle. It's the uncertainty of life that often can lead us into the fog without a clue as to where we're going. Because in uncertainty we can feel insecure.

It's the old Chinese farmer parable as told by one of my favorite philosophers, Alan Watts:

> Once upon a time there was a Chinese farmer whose horse ran away. That evening, all of his neighbors came around to commiserate. They said, "We are so sorry to hear your horse has run away. This is most unfortunate." The farmer said, "maybe."
>
> The next day the horse came back bringing seven wild horses with it, and in the evening everybody came back and said, "Oh, isn't that lucky. What a great turn of events. You now have eight horses!" The farmer again said, "maybe."
>
> The following day his son tried to break one of the horses, and while riding it, he was thrown and broke his leg. The neighbors then said, "Oh, dear, that's too bad," and the farmer responded, "We'll see."

The next day the conscription officers came around to conscript people into the army, and they rejected his son because he had a broken leg. Again all the neighbors came around and said, "Isn't that great!" Again, he said, "Maybe."

He goes on to explain that the whole process of nature is an integrated process of immense complexity, and it's impossible to tell whether anything that happens in it is good or bad—because you never know what will be the consequences of the misfortune or you never know what will be the consequences of good fortune.

I'm a believer in staying even keel when the seesaw moves up or down. At the same time celebrate the ups, celebrate what's present in our lives, and when it swings down, also remember what's present and that there's always gold somewhere. Ultimately, recognize that every moment is transient.

The most uncomfortable times of my life enabled me to see this world in a new way for the better. These difficult experiences have blossomed into also finding the good in moments of life, whether I feel on top or not. Because the contrast from discomfort has made me appreciate the comfortable moments so much more. It's made me understand the importance of these comfortable moments because I now understand how quickly they can be pulled from me. Not in a fearful state but a grateful state of presence.

There are days where it's very difficult to manage this mentality. Days where our emotions and human frailty will just pop up seemingly out of our control. And that's okay. We're weird little emotional creatures roaming a massive marble called earth floating in an infinite black space filled with black holes, other galaxies, and possibly other lifeforms. As big as our breakdowns may feel, I don't think it's as big as our physiological response makes it. Honestly, from this vantage point it goes back to this comedic tragedy we're in.

Sometimes the gold I've mined is a pat on the back. What is a better feeling than getting out to the other side of the fire? Where we can say to

CHAPTER SEVEN

AFTER THE GOLD

"I don't believe everything happens for a reason. But I do believe that if I'm still here, I have to make it mean something."

—Fallon Farinacci, Episode 204

Finding the gold doesn't mean the work is done.

During the original gold rush in 1848, no one struck gold and said, "Alright! Let's head home; I'm hungry." They staked their claim, hands got dirty, and they figured out what to do with it. The discovery was just the beginning—not the ultimate payoff.

And, just like finding the gold in discomfort, a louder question follows you out of the fire: *What now?*

We won't go back to who we were, we don't know how to move forward, and we're afraid of doing it wrong.

It's not solved with a strict plan or big movements. It's curated through small maneuvers in the way we live.

The word *legacy* is a bitch.

And, I've always felt a surge of what my life would add up to after my father's death. It churned into a subconscious decision-maker in everything I did. I wanted to live for my dad and turn my life into something meaningful so when people looked back on it they know that I left something behind in his honor.

It's one of those words that sounds noble but carries weight. The kind you don't notice at first until six months later someone pinches your lower belly fat. Legacy can be inspiring and paralyzing at the same time. It can take us from the present moment by focusing too much on the finish line and forgetting the steps that precede our arrival. Motivating and suffocating. It asks you to live well while quietly whispering, "Don't mess this up."

I thought legacy was something I had to live up to and look back on. Something eternal beyond my existence. But, the truth is legacy is in the here and the now, not in the focus of what the result will be.

I realized it isn't something we have to build after grief. Grief inherently stamps this idea of legacy immediately because it's such a big piece of our timeline. It's really how grief changes the way we live that ends up being our legacy.

When someone you love dies, they leave an imprint. And, when we lose this person, it offers the chance to contemplate our own imprint. It gives us a chance to examine how we're going to move forward. It shows up whether you invite it or not. It doesn't knock. It doesn't wait until you're ready. It just moves in and starts rearranging the furniture like a roommate we never wanted.

Every year on the anniversary of my father's death, I get those text messages. Thoughtful ones. Messages that say, "I'm thinking of you." I'm grateful for them. Truly. But for a long time, receiving them came with an unexpected side effect: guilt. A quiet question hiding behind the kindness. *Is this my legacy? Am I honoring him correctly?*

That question followed me for years.

As the 12-year-old "man of the house," I was starring in a role I never auditioned for. The self-inflicted responsibility to live in my father's wake. I didn't resist it. I absorbed it. There wasn't an instruction manual. Just a quiet understanding that everything had shifted and *what now?*

At the time, it didn't feel like an obligation as much as it felt like inheritance. A passing from one to another.

Only later did I realize how much responsibility I had unconsciously tied to that moment. Responsibility not just to help my family, but to *mean something.* To live in a way that honored the loss. To make my father proud—wherever proud people go when they die.

For a long time, I thought legacy was something I had to build. Something big. Something worthy of explanation. I thought it was my job to turn tragedy into purpose, pain into proof. That if I didn't do something meaningful enough with my life, I'd be failing not just myself—but him.

That kind of thinking sneaks up on you. It disguises itself as motivation. But underneath it is. Pressure to perform your healing correctly. Pressure to live loudly enough to give meaning to the loss. Pressure to turn grief into gold when it just looks like rusted iron.

And grief doesn't need help being heavy. It's already heavy as shit.

Legacy, as I first understood it, felt like permanence. It feels like a monument that would be viewed and judged by all at the end of my life. It made me feel frozen at times—afraid to choose a path, scared it'd be the wrong decision, forgetting the present moment. I was afraid to waste the life I still had, afraid that missteps would somehow dishonor the one I lost.

What I didn't understand yet was that legacy wasn't asking me to *do more.*

It was asking me to *pay attention*.

Only now have I come to realize it's not about figuring out *what I will leave behind*. It's more about how I live *now*.

Because ultimately, focusing on how we can live now will determine what we will leave behind.

LEGACY ISN'T WHAT WE LEAVE BEHIND, IT'S HOW WE LIVE NOW

For a long time, I thought legacy was something I had to build—something big and lasting. Something that would prove I had done something meaningful with the life I was still living for those not. This pressure clouds the way we move through life.

Then there was something that shifted this innate strain entirely: our imprint isn't something we create—it's something we pass through.

Grief has a way of stripping life down to its essentials. After you lose someone you love, the abstract idea of being remembered starts to feel less important than the very real question of *how you continue*.

Comedian Rodney Norman, who has lost two of his children, once put it this way: "A lot of people think staying miserable is how they prove their love. But another way to love someone is to live a great life and let them be part of your joy."

Living a great life after the worst moment of your life doesn't happen overnight. And, the overrated notion of legacy isn't assembled the same. It's to be looked at like going to the gym. Every repetition gets us closer to that six-pack but it takes time and intention.

When someone you love dies, their legacy doesn't fade as much as it coincides with our personal legacy. In the way we keep going. In the way we show up.

I didn't choose my father's legacy—it became part of me. His death didn't leave a void—it left an imprint. An imprint that shaped my decisions, my outlook, and, eventually, my work. I carried it for years without knowing what to do with it, mistaking responsibility for obligation.

It's not the size of our impact, but the consistency of our presence and how we show up every day. It's not a monument we leave behind. It's the little batons we leave with our living loved ones, strangers we pass in the street, and the way we interact with the world. The opposite of the cliché to "think big."

Think small.

Society glorifies the idea of leaving your mark—doing something big, unforgettable, worthy of applause. But letting go of that notion to do too much can be liberating. My perception of legacy shifted when I realized I don't need to live as if I'm preparing for applause. I need to live as if I'm preparing for memory.

That shift softened something in me.

Legacy stopped feeling like a show and started feeling like practice.

Kelly Carlin, who has lived much of her grief in the public eye, once described loss this way:

> "Death is a portal. It's a portal to the real life we're here to live . . . if you're willing to be taken apart by it, how you assemble yourself back together is going to be a much less conditioned way of being in the world."

Once grief pulls us apart, you don't get to go back to who you are. We only get to move forward into how we choose to put ourselves back together in the way we live.

It's a vibrating legacy catapulted by the way I want to live my life. An approach that relieved some of the pressure I'd been carrying by redirecting my attention to small, intentional actions.

Legacy, by definition, is a long-lasting impact. And if that's true, then grief itself creates legacy simply by enduring. If you're a griever, congratulations—you've had legacy thrust on you.

But what we do with that inheritance is where choice returns.

Continuing my dad's legacy has, in turn, shaped my own. Not by re-creating his life or living in his shadow, but by allowing his influence to move through me in subtle ways—patience, humor, presence. Legacy isn't frozen in the past; it's a way of life. It's built through movement and action.

Our impact is in our presence moment to moment.

This deliberate living is rarely heroic. It doesn't have to come with a headline in your local news for feeding a small town across the world. Most of the time, it looks like deciding not to be an asshole when you're frustrated with the world. Or it's in laughing and (for the first time) not feeling guilty about it. These little daily actions that may not feel important in the moment but it is crucial to the sum total of our life when each of these moments compound.

Cut yourself some slack trying to be extraordinary. Consistency of presence correlates to the size of the impact we make—no matter the size of the impact. Because it's not the size that matters, it's what we do with it. At least that's what I used to tell my ex-girlfriend.

Once I saw legacy this way, it stopped feeling heavy.

It started to feel light. Instead of having to carry all the groceries from the car to the front door in one trip I could just focus on one bag at a time.

My purpose and my legacy may very well be my podcast. Maybe. Then again, legacy is convoluted. It doesn't stop there. It's in the subtle maneuvers through life. And, my podcast is just one of many maneuvers.

The way I treat the server at a new restaurant even though they just overcooked my steak. The quick smile at a stranger that walks by offering a momentary acknowledgment that we both exist in passing nature. Showing up when my friends need me. Being the person who will drive you to the airport—unless it's rush hour, then I'm telling you to get an Uber.

It's the little things.

"72 CENTS. THAT'S HUGE. WHO KNEW?"

Penny Wittbrodt once told me a story on the show about the effect 72 cents can have. There was a woman in front of her in line at the grocery store one day who was 72 cents short of her bill. She began pulling items off the conveyor belt, quietly deciding what she could live without. Penny, a single mother herself, recognized the embarrassment and reached into her pocket to cover the difference.

At first, the woman refused. Pride kicked in. But Penny gently insisted, and eventually she accepted the help.

Years later, that same woman was working at a food pantry when another woman came in under similar circumstances—ashamed, apologetic, struggling. This time, she was on the other side of the counter. She reassured her. She helped her. The 72 cents had been passed through like a baton.

Before even getting into where that story came from, there's a lesson sitting right there. Our purpose or legacy is the million things we do every day. It may not feel big to us. But it might be everything to someone else.

It's the way we run through life and how we pass the metaphorical baton to others. Our legacy can live on through ripples in the ether—ripples we may never even witness.

Though I can't see my father anymore, he left behind multiple fractions of legacy. He was many things. But one thing he always sought was a laugh—and he usually got one. Humor, levity, amusement—those weren't distractions from life. They were part of how he lived it.

Without that, I don't think I'd be able to make it through. And maybe that's part of the real inheritance. Humor isn't just how we cope. It's how we live.

Legacy is an opportunity. It's not about how the world remembers you. It's about how you live each moment, how you love, how you show up, and how your presence creates a ripple effect for the people caught in your orbit. Which ultimately contradicts the first sentence in this paragraph. It's more a reframing of letting go of the end result and focusing on the little steps toward that end. It's that dash between our birth year and our death year.

You never know how your rhythm through life is changing the lives of others. Just because you can't see the impact doesn't mean it isn't there.

And for me, one of the clearest ways that legacy has continued to move through my life—one of the ways I've survived, reframed, healed, and stayed connected—is through humor.

CHAPTER EIGHT

LIFE IS A DARK COMEDY

"Humor isn't just a defense mechanism. It's a release."

—Dan Soder, Episode 202

I listened to the haunting beeping of a machine tracking my mother's heartbeat synchronized with the bass of my own heartbeat inside the intensive care unit (ICU) in Long Branch, New Jersey. The unaddressed trauma sat between my sisters and my mother's partner, Ken. In this moment we circle around my mother who was conscious for the first time after her cardiac arrest. We didn't think about long-term effects; we were just ecstatic that she was awake. She was communicating with us and sounding more like the woman we all knew and loved.

Aware of her depleted memory we eased into the conversations slowly, grateful that we have this moment with her. Her voice was raspy from the breathing tube but it was music to my ears. We reminded her that she was going to be a bit forgetful for a little while.

Somewhere along the way we mentioned Ken's name casually and my mother looked confused. She said Ken's name in the form of a question. The air was sucked from the room as I glanced at my sisters telepathically thinking the same thing, "Holy shit, she doesn't remember Ken." The only man she's been in love with since my father and has been by her side for decades at this point. Ken was on my left and I could almost feel his heart sink.

We were silent for a long few seconds before she slowly turned her head to look at Ken. She gave a weak smirk and an evil raspy laugh, completing either the greatest or worst joke in ICU history by pretending to have forgotten who Ken was. We all exhaled with relief and burst out in laughter. Although Ken may not have found it funny, my sister secretly slapped me and stopped laughing so hard. It was the levity we all needed. It was the perfect release of the tensest couple days of my life thinking I would lose my mom as well.

The beauty of laughter, even in times it does not optically seem suitable, is a beautiful asset to this thing called life.

If you're not in a place to read a dark humanistic approach then perhaps skip this chapter. At the same time don't skip it. We aren't meant to always agree with every approach out there. Just like every joke isn't for everyone.

I've often heard how humor can be a defense mechanism. And perhaps it was at some point for me. A way to deflect painful thoughts or experience. A tactic to avoid facing the repercussions of reality. I've discovered it can also be an offense mechanism.

As comedian Marc Maron has put it, humor takes things that are complicated and horrifying and simplifies them. It can make us see things in a totally new way and have a laugh at it. As he's said, "it's a beautiful necessary thing."

It set the stage of life for me as a dark comedy.

When people find out that my father died in the World Trade Center, it's as certain as death is, that they'll sympathetically say, "I'm so sorry." I instinctively react to break the tension and ask them, "It's okay; you didn't fly the plane into his building."

Now, I understand that isn't the most well-written joke of all time, but it's in my nature to ease the tension. A lot of people may find that distasteful. And, first, I'd like to acknowledge that it was my father and I'm deeply integrated into the story of September 11, so I wrote my own pass to make whatever jokes I want. Deal with it.

Second, it's an act of not only disarming the seriousness of this event but also the person I'm talking with. It turns down the dial of a touchy subject and shows that I'm okay with dialogue and grappling with the darkest parts of life. Not that I haven't had awkward moments; I have, but fortunately for me, I thrive in awkwardness. That's just a part of my sick sense of humor when I'm my own audience.

Once, I was smoking a cigarette outside of a local bar and sparked a conversation with two strangers. It's Los Angeles so it takes 37 seconds before someone asks what you do for a living. After sharing that I talk about death for a living the young woman naturally asked why I talk about death. So, I told her "Bin Laden." After I allowed an awkward few seconds to pass by I clarified that my father died on 9/11. Thinking my response would relieve her apparent stress just made it worse. She gave me the predictable "I'm so sorry" and I followed with my predictable "It's okay; you weren't flying the plane." That was my cue to put out my cigarette, leave, and stick with my friends who can handle this distasteful humor in the eyes of society.

This life is out of control. It often makes no sense even when we think we're making sense of it. Horrible things happen to a point where I don't know what else to do but throw my hands up and say, "Welp!" It's a cliché, but laughter really is the best medicine.

It's made what we call reality lighter. It takes a load off even if it's momentary. And it's a reminder that I can find joy within the most dimly lit moments of life. Even when it's brief, we can forget the world and just for a blink things are alright.

Sometimes the timing is completely off, and I've offended people at my own expense. So, that's been a bit of a learning curve of knowing when to crack jokes. But it's been my savior and I'll be this way for the rest of my life.

I had a chat with comedian Dan Soder, who lost his father at 14, and also his step-sister, who was his biggest support system. He had one of those complicated grief scenarios because he was abandoned by his father whom he always had love for. A lot of his grief that he's had to work out for decades is the relationship with his dad that he had *while he was alive*. The entire tone of his storytelling was beautifully mixed with reality of his experience and disarming humor.

"People act like humor is a defense mechanism, and maybe it starts that way. But at some point, it just becomes a way to handle the absurdity of life."

As we tapped into my story of 9/11, he told me he was jealous of how my father died. "Whenever I met someone whose dad died in 9/11, I was kinda jealous. Like, dude, you have a historical moment for your grief. My dad just died in a rundown bowling alley bar."

He's saying that to my face. And some people cringe at that. But when you go deeper it simplifies the complicated, horrifying death and complex relationship he experienced. His dad was an alcoholic and killed himself by going to bars. He reflected on the sad truth that his father didn't die in a way that brought any closure. And levity is his way of handling the absurdity of it all.

Humor isn't always a deflection; it's an acknowledgment of pain that can make it bearable. Grief doesn't go away completely—but laughing with it makes it a bit more tolerable. Just like the art of making a joke is founded in comedic timing, there are times where we need to be sensitive to certain situations out of compassionate respect to others.

So, when someone is grieving you may need to dial it down and just be supportive.

If making jokes isn't in your make-up, then there is another angle to consider—merely that it is okay to laugh. This isn't about being the jokester but giving yourself permission to laugh. If you're watching your favorite movie, show, or one of your friends trips and falls, you can take those 15 seconds to belly laugh. The laughter amid pandemonium is the point. It's a reprieve.

Not to be a buzzkill, but as hopeful as these moments can be, there's a level of self-awareness required in how we approach them. Senses of humor are not created equally. There is a bit of a radar system to be wary of to know if you're on the defense or offensive side of this medicine.

TO COPE OR AVOID

If I had a nickel for every time someone has told me my dark humor is a defense mechanism I'd probably have a penthouse suite in downtown Manhattan by now.

But I've read that when we laugh, our brains release a cocktail of neurotransmitters and hormones that include dopamine, serotonin, and endorphins. Now, unless you're a robot, I don't think you need scientific evidence that laughter makes you feel good. It's like an untied balloon filled to the max in which each giggle releases a little bit of air relieving some pressure. It may not release the air pressure in one belly laugh, but it certainly helps. We can gauge this by how we feel right after a chuckle.

The laugh medicine doesn't stop as a physical sensation. It can relieve anxiety, reduce tension, and provide a temporary escape from the reality of emotions and certain situations. Our trauma really messes up our physiology. I see humor as a chiropractor getting everything in line in a way that disperses the difficult reality.

LAUGHITATION THERAPY

Past guest and comedian Craig Shoemaker tapped into how laughter can be healing, "Laughter is a vibration and a frequency that can break through the dams of grief."

He was kidnapped, his wife joined a cult, he lost one of his best friends, and he attempted to take his own life. After Craig told me the story about how he tried to hang himself with neckties he showed me a touch of his comedic timing for the listeners, "Do you see advertisements for neckties now? Because you will."

Craig created the Laughter Heals Foundation, which promotes the awareness of the powerful healing properties that laughter and music have for our physical, mental, spiritual well-being, and for the health of our relationships.

Laughter is not a trivial notion—it's a vital tool for survival and healing. His story balances vulnerability that let me into darkness that was broken from the light of laughter. Demonstrating that humor is a secret weapon to reclaiming our life.

He took me through a process he calls *guided laughitation,* which is a practice like anything else. The core of it is forcing ourselves to laugh. Not at a specific joke, not necessarily real laughter to start, but to physically go through the act of laughing while simultaneously talking about something traumatic. I'd highly recommend checking out our podcast episode 108 in which we exercised this technique step-by-step. Because reading it may make us look even crazier than we did on camera.

Craig initiates. "Watch how it works. You just laugh along with me. Here we go."

Craig starts to maniacally laugh out loud, signaling that I join him. So, at this point we're both letting out initially unauthentic belly laughs.

He then shouts mid-laughter, "My wife joined a cult!," more laughter ensues as he delivers each emotional line.

"She moved out in the middle of the night and took the kids!"

More forced laughter comes out from both of us to the point where my discomfort during this process dissolves and now feels like I am authentically laughing.

"I came back from a trip, expecting her to pick me up at the airport. She said, 'Read your email!' I'm out of here!" Even more bursts of laughter progressed until we were both red in the face.

At the end, Craig stops laughing and directs me to breathe through my nose and let out a long "ahhh." He takes a beat and checks in on how I feel.

I felt completely relaxed as if I just went through a therapy session. He said "It doesn't mean anything when you're saying this and expressing it in a way that's positive and a positive vibration. It doesn't mean anything except for being in the now. Now you're present. You're aware. You're hanging with me. We're having fun. And that's how it works. That's what laughter can do."

It's a refocus on how it's the *laughter* that is important, not necessarily the comedy. The physical manifestation of it coming out of our body resulted in a needed emotional release. This practice accesses laughter without the agenda of a joke.

Avoidance can make the pain worse. It's trying to hold that beach ball underwater. When we avoid our grief it's because it is hard and we think we're protecting ourselves. Laughing is just one of many tools that enables us to *move the energy* and not keep it tucked away. And that laughing does not mean forgetting or shoving the pain aside. It means living in spite of it, or with it.

Laughter doesn't make grief disappear, but it makes life *with grief* more livable.

Take a second to force yourself to laugh for a few moments. Maybe do it when you're alone or at least give the person you share a house with a heads up so they don't think you're morphing into the Joker. But give it a shot. Force some laughter in the face of your pain. Break through that discomfort at first and fully let go allowing yourself to be in this moment of action. At minimum give yourself the authorization to keep your humor antennae extended with permission to laugh when the grief comes. When we find ourselves laughing for the first time it's a reflection of the "normality" of the way things were.

This practice of laughter and humor has helped me not only cope but also connect. After this ruthless icebreaker it shows the person on the other side that I'm comfortable with it. When my guard is down then it often lets the guard down with the other person and we start to have a dialogue.

We can have the courage and grit to drop the shield and feel the pain in order to move forward. Avoidance is just an Advil. It keeps you away from the pain from the headache but in another few hours you'll need to take another. By facing the core of it all we can take strides to mitigate more headaches in the future with our natural pharmacy.

HUMOR IS AN X VARIABLE

Whether it's a wildly inappropriate 9/11 joke or disappearing into the gym, humor in this chapter is simply the *x* in the equation. Fill in the *x* with whatever makes sense in your life.

Avoidance activities show up in every possible flavor outside of grief-related knock-knock jokes. The key is *awareness:* noticing how you feel and how your tendencies are influencing that. Sometimes the people closest to you notice your patterns before you do—they're a barometer. But eventually the responsibility comes back to you.

I know people that are total meatheads—beautiful people, but meatheads, nonetheless. When something triggers them, they go lift 4,000 pounds to escape the feeling. On paper, the gym is healthy and of course there are benefits. But it can also be a mask to avoid the roar.

An activity can be healthy *and* still be avoidance if we're using it to dodge something essential. You don't need to stop a healthy or productive thing. You just need to make sure you're not using it to ignore a hurting part of yourself.

Contrast that with the people who go to the gym (or whatever your *x* variable is) consistently because it grounds them, helps them process, keeps them connected to their body, and supports their mental health.

Same action.

Different intention.

Different internal impact.

I used the punching bag to release some energy in the form of a physical release. I didn't feel like I was running away from my emotions because the next day I'd watch the footage. It's an ebb and flow from activity to activity to attend to different needs.

Some people bury themselves in work. And honestly? That's fine . . . to a point. I'm all for temporary escapes that don't need this existential intention if it helps you catch your breath. I believe those are necessary too—brainless activities that just give you a damn break from reality. That's part of my process, too. But stay buried too long and you lose the map back to yourself.

Work can also provide connection, creativity, expression, and community. Again: same action, different intention, different outcome.

That's why this whole topic is an *x* variable. The specifics change from person to person, but the principle is constant. A little accountability goes a long way.

The question is rarely, "Is this good or bad?"

The question is "What is this doing for me right now?"

Because filling in your *x* might be a trauma response. Filling in your *x* may be a beneficial response. You might not even realize you're doing it with either direction. We're all capable of going on autopilot while our emotions sit in the backseat waving a flare. And sometimes we *have* to do that.

But at some point, we could ask *Are we coping or are we avoiding?*

And I truly believe if we sit back deep enough we all know which is which when we decide to be honest with ourselves.

Reactions are automatic. Responses are learned. And, with learned responses our reactions can change or we can be quicker to catch our responses. The gap between the two—that beat, that pause that choice—is where growth lives. You will always react. You're human. But over time, you start catching yourself mid-reaction and choosing differently.

That's the practice.

That's the rewiring.

When I try to improve my own responses, I do it by examining the feeling, not the story I've attached to the feeling. I ask myself whether my *x* variable is helping me or helping me hide.

None of this requires self-judgment. In fact, judgment only muddies the water. I try to detach myself from my own biases and self-loathing for reacting a certain way. It's a release of being so hard on myself when I don't respond in the way I wanted or have been practicing. It's almost an "I'll get 'em next time" mentality, and that's the learning process.

I get frustrated when I find my emotions tangled up in my reactions. But when I sprinkle in a little logic through the emotional static, I remember this is part of the process of just being human. We're beautifully flawed. And I'd even retract the word flawed and just stick to we're human. Not because life is binary, but because a little simplicity can make the chaos easier to navigate.

And yes . . . I'm aware none of this is funny in a chapter about the importance of humor. Maybe that's the ironic joke. So, before I make one of my ill-timed jokes, let's return to the power of levity by visiting a place where humor and death coexist in the most unexpected ways.

SĂPÂNȚA'S MERRY CEMETERY

There's a place in the world where humor doesn't tiptoe around death—it walks right up to it, cracks a joke, paints it bright blue, and sticks it on a headstone.

The Merry Cemetery in Săpânța, Romania, is known for its vibrant tombstones that blend humor with the commemoration of the deceased. This interesting tradition was initiated by local woodcarver Stan Ioan Pătraș in 1935, who began crafting colorful crosses adorned with witty epitaphs and art depicting the lives of those buried there. The writings often include very blunt and humorous reflections on the deceased, which offers a lighthearted perspective on death.

If you were to walk these grounds, you'd see an eclectic expression of vibrant colors including its signature shade called Săpânța blue, which symbolizes hope and freedom. I found depictions that are rather macabre illustrating violent imagery representing the way the person had died, such as car accidents. While if you were to further explore you might see artistic expressions of something lighter and more peaceful. And all throughout you'd find witty poetic inscriptions that might make you smile.

One epitaph from the tombstone of a mother who had died said this:

Underneath this heavy cross
Lies my mother-in-law poor
Had she lived three days more
I'd be here and she would read
You that are passing by
Try not to wake her up
For she comes back home

She'll bite my head off
But I'll act in the way
That she will not return
Stay here my dear
Mother-in-law.

After discovering this tradition, it made me wonder if I lived a past life in Romania. This cultural attitude toward death not only embraces our mortality with humor but in that creates a form of acceptance. This burial ground gives us a lighthearted perspective of life and death, completely splitting away from a more traditional view of solemnity.

It's an eclectic paradigm shift of perspectives that this community has embraced. With the magic touch of humor comes a new perspective that can shine light on a different viewpoint in a way. More important, it's unique to the individual or family regardless of how the outside world perceives it. These grounds are a perfect example because even through humor the intention is to honor the ones we lost.

The Merry Cemetery to me represents humor, just one part of a complex topography. In my world, humor opens the door for out-of-the-box thinking. It creates a new outlook that decompresses the pressure of grief—even if just for a moment. I've come to realize that in the depths of pain those momentary releases offer hope and a new processing system. This cemetery encompasses that though humor is a part of this tradition, it's not the whole. It's attached to expression, remembrance, honesty, acceptance, and a new perspective.

That's what humor is to me. It's a catalyst. And, like the individual recipes of our life it comes in many forms.

Dan Soder compared his father to the protagonist of the horror film *The Shining*. He made a joke about how Jack Nicholson's character, Jack Torrence, was a better father in that film than his father. It's a humorous angle of the truth. He had to come to terms that his father wasn't a good father at all and that was part of his grief process. By laying it down as a ridiculous metaphor it removes pressure from his reality but also faces the dark truth that is pivotal to his healing.

Laughing in the face of death to me isn't a form of disrespect; it's a form of taking control in an uncontrollable world. A moment where the pressure is released gives me hope and is a reminder that there is still joy to be found. When I die, I want to be roasted, not eulogized.

And, frankly, the people who have gone through the most difficulty in life tend to have the best sense of humor. That's not a coincidence.

I've learned through terrible jokes at the wrong time that there are moments to talk and moments to shut up. In my circle, there are no limits. I'm surrounded by people who have gone through it. And part of our process of getting through it is to laugh our way through it because it opens the door for the mucky stuff to come out through confronting it.

Truth is part of this process too and finding the humor often can reveal that truth. The truth can come from someone else and most important it has to come from within ourselves to ourselves. And, when the world is burning all around us and things get dangerous you better get ready for a wise-ass comment that might just distract you from the flames. That diversion is not only a temporary relief but it's also leaving a door ajar for a new way to see things. Humor doesn't erase the pain—it simply illuminates it differently.

CHAPTER NINE

OTHER VIEWS

"Your perspective is not the only perspective."

—Sah D'Simone, Episode 122

Every major loss feels like being dropped into another galaxy. One minute you're living in the world you know—the next, gravity feels different. People move differently. Food tastes different. Even silence sounds deafening. The old world seems to die with them, and suddenly, you're living in a place you never asked to visit.

Suddenly, our views on everything change. Our views on ourselves, the world, the people in it, and often our views on the unseen mechanics of the world and why we're here. It's important to know that our perspectives continually shift and change. And just because you have been thrown into a dimension you don't want to be in, it becomes more important to focus on how we see things.

I've heard over and over that people who are in deep grief say that "it never gets better." I wholeheartedly disagree. There seems to be a confusion between "better" meaning fully healed or back to the way we were. They're not the same.

I broke my hand playing rugby in college and my hand has never been the same. It was excruciating for a while. It took physical therapy to get it stronger. I now have metal in my hand and a scar that reminds me of the break. But it got better. Better doesn't mean fixed; it simply means progress or growth.

The point is the scar will always be there. And, if we have control of anything it's how we look at our visible and invisible scars.

I don't do well with negativity. I have an incredible belief in the human spirit because I've experienced it. I've seen it time and time again with people that have persevered through some of life's biggest challenges. The words we speak carry energy that creates the reality around us. That reality around us is shaped by the way we view life. And, just as our views shift after facing death in life it can shift in any direction we want with effort.

I believe that.

This isn't an overnight adaptation. When you start going to the gym do you look in the mirror in two weeks and stop working out because you don't have a six pack? Then when you look in six months you haven't quite got the six pack, but maybe some more definition. It's a process. It's a marathon. It's the little things we do that compound into improvement.

This mantra isn't just a flip of a switch. It's hiring a bad electrician, changing the light bulbs, and after enough trial and error the light finally came on. Or at least, it flickered.

I'm not here to sell you hope. If anything, I'm here to present the possibility. That's not up to me. If you believe it will never get better, then it probably won't. If you believe it can get better, then it might. If you believe it will get better, then it probably *will*.

Heck, you can even just say maybe! At least leave that possibility door ajar.

If my story sucks and isn't inspiring you enough, this is where I go to plan B. To the other views of people and cultural perspectives that have helped me reform my perception of life by being open-minded to the *maybe*.

THE LYON'S DEN

Lyon Herron was diagnosed with a rare genetic disease and battled cancer for 27 years before dying at the age of 31.

I spoke to his mother, Barbie, three months after his death. I couldn't help but feel the warmth in her soul despite the recent death of Lyon. I was eager to understand her perspective on her family's experience to be able to carry on in such a beautiful manner.

"I feel that he came here to show people how to live. And then at the end, he showed people how to die," Barbie told me. This hit me.

Lyon endured a life of suffering while Barbie and her family were by his side. She could have perceived his suffering in a million different ways and she settled on finding meaning in the suffering. Everything I've heard from the people who knew Lyon, as well as the stories Barbie told me, was that Lyon never saw himself as a victim and defined his own experience knowing he was going to die. During the suffering and after his death Barbie didn't express the "conventional" grief that one may expect from a grieving mother. Instead of feeling consumed by loss, she expressed courageous gratitude for having decades with her son. She faced his decline by having open discussions with him, which included laughter and raw emotions. "People would walk in and say, 'You look great!' and I'd say, 'No, you don't, honey. You're dying.' And we'd just wink and laugh."

They had a living memorial before he passed where their friends and family came to the house to celebrate his life. It came with the pain and the tears, but the perspective was built on commemoration. Barbie perceives death as a part of a large sacred journey.

This family's journey was part of changing the perception of death. Barbie told me, "If we can remove the fear of dying, the world would be way less scary." She could've easily been mad at the world. Question the heavens as to why her inspiring son lived a life of suffering. She could have taken a completely different path. Instead she made a choice to carry the weight in a way that continues life.

"We are the ones left behind, so we have a choice in how we carry our grief. I choose to carry it with gratitude and love."

This is Barbie's story, not a prescription, just a reminder that other views exist. It doesn't have to be applied to your life's GPS. But it doesn't hurt to contemplate detours and see if there's another route that may get to your destination with fewer stop signs.

Talking with Barbie made me realize that acceptance doesn't mean detachment. It means staying open—even in heartbreak. And then I met someone who embodied a similar openness in a completely different way. Where Barbie found peace through letting go, Gabriella found life by holding on.

PAIN TO PURPOSE

When legendary actor Gary Sinise came on the show in 2025 to have a chat with me about losing his son Mac to a rare spinal cancer in early 2024, his entire life was upended. It was a test of faith and a capacity for love, all of which was expressed in grief. And through the grief, Gary discovered something profoundly human: that service and storytelling can become the lifeline when pain threatens to consume you.

Not long after his son died, Gary began to share Mac's story publicly for the first time. He expressed that he wasn't seeking sympathy, but he did it to extend the same message he has preached to the veterans his foundation services: *tell your story*.

For years, the Gary Sinise Foundation has supported soldiers struggling to share their experiences not only as a form of self-healing but also as an act of service to inspire and help others going through similar experiences. Now, in his own grief, Gary found that same act just as applicable.

Speaking about his son's fight, courage, and his grief experience not only became a memorial but also a medicine.

He described his grief as something you *manage*, not something time simply heals. "Time doesn't heal all wounds," he said. "But you learn how to manage." He's not romanticizing the experience of loss but expressing how in managing we find ways to carry it without letting it paralyze you. For him, sharing stories is not necessarily relieving pain but releasing it.

Gary found meaning in the action of serving no matter how grand the gesture. Our service to the world and to everyone we interact with can restore a sense of purpose when grief seemingly takes that away. "Service is a great healer," he said. "When you do something to make someone else smile, it changes their day . . . and yours."

In service and talking about his son's death, he never denied the weight of sorrow. He doesn't express there isn't still weight there or that it will ever go away, fully. He acknowledges moments of guilt, the wish for a future gone, and the waves of emotions that come without warning. But he did allow these emotions to come and go freely.

This outlook that grief can break you open in ways that reveal the humanness behind us all. And, how service, love, storytelling are not distractions from the pain but extensions of it. He lives as a father in mourning and man in motion using what opened him up to help others hold what's breaking them.

BOTH SIDES OF LIFE AND DEATH

"Life gets better no matter what, even if it takes 10 years to get there."

Pretty wise and optimistic words from a youthful human. Magician and escapist Gabriella Lester lost her teenage boyfriend to suicide and attempted to take her own life. She laid down the groundwork that no matter how dark life gets, there's power in choosing to keep living side by side with the pain.

She said, "It's okay to live and grieve at the same time. You don't have to wait for the hard thing to be completely over before you keep living." These words are indicative of life. One could argue that suffering is a constant in life. Through Gabriella's lens, her only certainty is seeing *life* as a certainty, and the importance of focusing on making the most of it even while simultaneously in the thick of it.

Her perspective of carrying through with hope and a choice to believe that life *will* get better as opposed to my notion of saying that it *can*. It reminds us to be more vigilant on what we focus on because what we focus on manifests into action.

In Gabriella's case, this didn't seem like a perspective she was just born with. It was learned and practiced. It was absorbed through her own grief and turmoil in life to choose this attitude by looking at things in a different way. This is why I want to challenge the world to just *look*. I'm not saying it has to be this way or that way. But just take a peek at the labyrinth of possibilities in this world and maybe you'll be surprised at the way the universe speaks to us.

Life is rarely black and white. Our initial viewpoint doesn't have to be our final viewpoint. Any viewpoint doesn't have to be our eternal viewpoint. They can be malleable. Within the malleability is possibility. Perspective to me is a flexible tool that we can shift while also we striving toward building a foundation with it. The event that we're rebounding from is fixed but our thoughts don't have to be. And it's often the fuel to any shocking turn of events where your one day will make a sharp turn upwards just from one simple realization that we never considered before.

Gabriella's choice to keep living through her grief felt like an act of rebellion in a sense. But Grace took that defiance a step further. She didn't just live *with* loss—she lived with death staring right at her.

A TICKING TIME BOMB

Grace Wethor was 13 years old when the doctors told her she had six months to live. They found an inoperable brain tumor and offered no outlook on how to manage it. When she was 23, she came on my show, still here, to share her story, describing her tumor as a "ticking time bomb." To date, there's no explanation as to how she is still alive and what her future looks like. Grace has had to live day by day since she was just a young girl.

She explained to me that she's shifted her perspective of how she defines the tumor. "I took the context that's traditionally perceived with a brain tumor—that's so horrible, that's so bad—and replaced it with my own. When I thought of it, I thought of community, joy, and opportunity."

It's as simple as that. She created her own definition with a new perception. It curated a deep growth in her darkest experience knowing that at any moment things could change. And, despite this seemingly simplistic perspective shift, it doesn't happen overnight. It's taken her years. But, as she puts it, she just did *something*.

Irrespective of being certain she was going in the right direction, she kept moving. She drove through the fear of living and the fear of dying by continuing to live. And this process of doing *something* one frame at a time through small actions led to how she sees life now. It's choosing action in the face of it all.

I said to her in our discussion that it was almost like her tumor was a superpower. It's led her to chase all her dreams. It's led her to make the most of every day and live a compassionate life realizing that everyone has a metaphorical tumor because we often don't know what others are going through. I said to her, "Sometimes I feel like life is a ticking time bomb in many ways, because you don't know when that bomb's going to go off—with or without a tumor."

Grace turned her six-month diagnosis into a launching pad for her dreams that has turned into books, public speaking, and working with legislators to help build awareness for pediatric cancer. She could have easily stayed in bed. Instead, she chose motion and action to make the best of the cards she was dealt. This is her intentional choice to see life this way.

In the early days of Grace's diagnosis, her mother said, "You can be sad, but you can't be sad for too long." It's okay to have flare-ups of sadness throughout life but it's about not staying there. Creating a life beyond sadness is possible. She's shown me that it is possible to learn when and how to carry it by "acknowledging the sadness but not being imprisoned by it."

Grace reminded me that our time here is unpredictable—and maybe that's the very thing that makes it sacred. It's why I've stopped trying to make sense of death and allow it to teach me about being alive.

MOVING WHILE TERRIFIED

After hearing stories like Barbie's, Gabriella's, and Grace's, I started to realize that perspective doesn't stop at how we live through grief—it extends all the way to how to live our lives—through acceptance, gratitude, coexistence, and courage.

Barbie taught me about acceptance and gratitude in loss, Gabriella taught me how to live and grieve at once, and Grace taught me how to be courageous in the face of uncertainty. Together, they reframed the way I see living itself.

Through acceptance and gratitude, we can find meaning in suffering. Through coexistence we can live and hope while we grieve. Through courage in uncertainty we can reframe how we see things and act.

Perspective starts with how we choose to carry our pain. We don't get to choose our pain, but we do get to choose what we do with it. That's where gratitude and courage meet—in motion. It's saying, "I'll keep living, even when I don't want to." Because in the moments we least want to move, courage always extends its hand because that's our choice. We just have to grab it.

Perspective is the ignitor to action. It's saying I'll keep living even when I don't want to. It's in the "I don't want to" where courage reaches out for us. We just have to grab it, despite our body telling us not to. I choose to live with the unknown instead of waiting for certainty. The only certainty I know of is that life is uncertain.

I don't know how to remove fear, I only know how to move with fear. I used to think courage meant feeling fearless. Now I think it's moving while terrified. Every brave person I've met has told me they were scared shitless—they just kept going.

When I was in high school there was this one kid who was the toughest kid in town. I had this perception that he was fearless because he never backed down from anyone. I'll never forget after he got up and we were walking to the battlegrounds that he started to shake his body and said, "I always get so nervous before I'm about to beat someone's ass."

Aside from the morality of the action he embodied the notion that fear and courage aren't two separate entities. And even the seemingly bravest feel the same emotions of fear, anxiety or nerves that we all do. The difference is in the doing despite.

Life is movement. With movement we can explore a side of us we didn't know existed. I've found that the little movements are more important than the big movements because little movements compound. In my life these movements came from a mother who taught me to keep moving. It's evolved into throwing my hands up and admitting I have no idea what I'm doing at times, which is me facing life honestly. The more I explore the less I seem to know. And, after decades of thinking this way, I've been slower to anger, more understanding, and more accepting. Even in loss, perspective determines whether we stay stuck in what we lost or carry forward with what remains. And, what remains is life.

I don't know about you, but I don't want to feel like I'm dead while I'm alive.

I live within the mantra that *we're just figuring this shit out, man*. We live in a world that tells us how we're supposed to be from people who are still figuring it out, too. We inherit perspectives from parents, schools, strangers online—half the time we're living by rules someone else made up. Perspectives are placed on us from childhood and it's confusing to know what's ours. I've taken these hundreds of conversations and personal navigation of life to learn that plenty can be "taken" from me, but the way I choose to see things is forever mine.

We don't have to see things the same way. And, within these differences we can coexist in harmony understanding we all share the common bond of death.

Sometimes I go cross-eyed trying to make sense of it all, but maybe that's the point. These questions aren't meant to be answered; they're meant to make us see and feel differently. Perspective doesn't erase pain—it reframes it. And sometimes, that shift is enough to remind us that we're still alive, still learning, still here.

CHAPTER TEN

WHILE WE'RE ALIVE

"It's the difference between looking forward to it, or just dragging yourself through it."

—Dr. Gladys McGarey, Episode 175

You're still here—even if someone you love isn't.

This chapter isn't just about how to keep going after loss. It's about how to *live* while you're alive. Not just survive—but live—with purpose, with curiosity, with heart, and joy. Because whatever healing means it isn't only about grief—it's about learning how to be fully human, even when it hurts.

People ask me all the time—"Has your podcast helped you with your grief?" And I say, "Yes, of course." But not in the way they're probably thinking.

See, grief is tricky. It's not a five-step process like assembling IKEA furniture. Although, maybe it is like IKEA because it's a lot more than five steps, typically, and often screws are loose. It's more like wandering into a tornado with a plastic spoon and a mixtape, hoping for the best.

By the time I started the podcast, I'd been marinating in grief for two decades. It wasn't fresh. It was aged grief. The kind that's soft around the edges but still stings if you poke it. And I wasn't wallowing in it, either. I was just curious. About death. About life. About what the hell we're doing here besides eating too much processed food.

What I've learned—accidentally, mostly—is that talking about death is talking about life. It's the same damn thing wearing a different outfit.

Grief, as it turns out, is just life turned inside out. It's every emotion you've ever had tossed into a blender with the lid off. It's messy, weird, and kind of beautiful, in a "life's-a-joke-but-I'm-laughing-anyway" sort of way.

The people I've spoken with, the heartbreak they've endured, the strange, beautiful wisdom they've stumbled into after the worst days of their lives—it's changed me. It's changed how I show up. It's changed how I look at traffic, my reflections, and the people I love who still have a pulse.

The things grief teaches you are the same things that make you better at being alive. Being patient. Being kind. Knowing when to shut up. Knowing when to cry. And, realizing we know nothing. Laughing when your kid poops on your favorite shirt and realizing it's not the end of the world—it's just a Wednesday.

These conversations didn't just help me grieve—they've helped me live. Because when you talk about death long enough, you start to see life a little more clearly. If not clearer, it's made me look at life differently. You start to see what matters and what doesn't. Spoiler: most of it doesn't. So no, this isn't just for people who are grieving. It's for people who are breathing. Which is still you. For now.

If I ever used his death as an excuse to stop living my father would haunt me with that big wooden spoon from the kitchen. I'd hear it clanking through the hall at night. Not to scare me. Just to remind me: "You're still here, kid—don't waste it."

It's a blend of practical approaches to grief that I've absorbed as well as complete perspective shifts of how we find meaning in life.

Mr. Grief himself, David Kessler, said to me on the podcast, "Grieve fully and live fully. You can't just do one." This is the duality of healing after loss.

Grief and life work like a seesaw—one often outweighs the other—but finding balance, even if temporary, is where healing begins. I've yet to feel perfect balance and I'm not entirely sure life goes that way.

We go up, we go down, and sometimes flat on our face. When you're at your high, we may go down at some point. And, when you're down you must know we can swing back up at a moment's notice. And all levels complement each other because without one we don't know the other. It's the sweet in-between the highs and lows that reveal life.

It's not about perfecting the balance of the pendulum as it swings. It's about learning how to move with it. Finding a rhythm in the salsa of life—even if it feels like you've never taken a single dancing lesson.

For a long time, I didn't realize I was growing at all. I didn't feel anything largely noticeable. But, with that I knew something had shifted. I went from stuck to talking too much. Realizing that sometimes growth sounds like silence. Sometimes the most honest move is shutting up and saying less. As someone that talks for a living this has to also remain an option.

Jorge Perez, past guest and author of *The Shut The F*ck Up Method*, once said to me, "What's the cutoff between talking because it's healthy and talking because you're staying stuck?"

The answer isn't necessarily in the silence as much as it is an awareness to understand whether the talking stops creating space. And, whether anything else we're doing is overcrowding the space we fill.

The space where grief and life can coexist.

Living and grieving aren't opposites that have to exist on their own. They're companions. We don't have to choose one in order to have the other.

Some of us have managed our grief for so long that we've forgotten to let life back in. And, at the same time many have focused on living that they've pushed grief to the side. The work is figuring out how to hold both at the same time. After all, we have two hands.

Let go of perfecting this balance. And, be willing to keep aiming forward while remaining present. Shoot for the moon, they say. Even if you miss, you'll land among the stars. I say, even if you miss the stars, at least your view keeps expanding.

Which brings me back to permission. Give yourself permission to allow life back in. It doesn't mean diving headfirst into the deep end. Dip your toes in. And, it's okay to revert back because the water feels too cold. Dip them in again. Then your ankles. Then your shins. And, before you know it you're swimming again. Not because you're forced to do any of this. But because you've stopped seeing the water as an eternal threat.

"Living fully" is unique to you as it is unique to the billions of other people gravitationally stuck on this planet. It requires an intentional and decisive maneuver to *choose* to reengage with life even when it feels difficult. This does not mean that we ignore the grief. Allow the pendulum to swing while you're living.

Living fully to me means being authentically me. And letting the rest fall into place. The part that makes it a little convoluted is that I'm continually learning about myself while I concurrently examine my life.

If I feel my goals align with who I know I am then I'm living my life fully. This book felt authentic, and sometimes when writing I catch myself overthinking what the reader wants. Although I am writing this for the reader I am also writing it for myself and have to remind myself if I keep my voice authentic then it'll be the best experience possible. If the book sucks while maintaining myself within the lines, then well, maybe I'm just a shit writer.

By keeping true to ourselves whether that be with our humor, our choices, the way we engage with humans, the way we style our home or whatever it may be—we give those around us a better experience. If we're constantly trying to live, trying to grieve for others then we're doing those still living and those dead a disservice.

You can't please everybody. And, if being authentically me loses some people along the way, then was it ever authentic to begin with?

Experiencing deep grief in your life can bring out the worst in you. Sometimes the worst in you is still being authentic because that's where you are right now.

However I grieve and however I live, I'm going to be David. It's so much freer that way. The rest will fall into place once we lock in our interior world and self-confidence. When I found this authentic rhythm I felt I could be more vocally expressive. It allowed me to create more vulnerable conversations in my personal life and on my podcast.

It's a balance of not rushing wherever you are right now. Trust your own clock. Or turn it off. That's living fully and grieving simultaneously. Much easier said than done, but what the hell is easier said than done, anyway?

Often, it feels like we may never find the balance. But it's the engagement to find balance that ignites the fire of finding life again if you feel like you've lost it or never had it. That engagement can start in small increments. I ask of you to continue to emphasize this engagement as completely subjective. The intentional authenticity is my focus and works for me. It may not be your recipe. Tweak it. Add your spin to it or perhaps try something completely different. I just implore you to explore different things to find what works for you.

My mother may give me a delicious recipe for meat lasagna. After making it, trying it, and following her strict instructions on how much salt to add, this much mozzarella (mootz-a-rella not motz-a-rella) I realize . . . you know what? I like a little less salt and double the amount of cheese. And that works for me. I can share the same recipe to my other friend who is a vegetarian. She might keep all the ingredients the exact same except substitute the meat for zucchini. And this recipe is what works for her. My podcast has become my therapy, though there was a time I took the traditional approach.

There was only one time in my life I tried therapy. I had about two sessions. To no surprise, the therapist I was assigned told me he was retiring. How absurd is that? I always jokingly say "I'm so messed up that I caused a therapist to call it quits." Sweet.

Perhaps I didn't find the right person but nevertheless I didn't resonate with it. Maybe it is because of the bouncing boards I have in my life to talk to or who will just listen. I think my podcast has been a massive form of therapy for me. This is what I found. I could have sought another therapist beyond the old wrinkly one I sent to Boca Raton but I didn't. I listened to myself and didn't feel the need. Yet, I'm open to changing my mind and keeping my radar engaged should someone else cross my path, and it feels right, try again. I'm not closing doors, I'm opening new ones and keeping some cracked open.

Outside of lasagna, grief (life) is just like cooking—no one recipe works for everyone. Some need more salt (tough love), others more sugar (self-compassion). Sometimes you need to throw the whole damn dish you just cooked in the trash and start over. Sometimes you don't even feel like cooking. The key is figuring out what combination of ingredients works for you because at the end of the day, we all have to eat.

I started with a cup of red cayenne pepper in the form of a punching bag, which has transmuted now into only a tablespoon in the form of working out at the gym instead of bleeding my knuckles. For dessert, I'll always have my 100% pure cacao. These are just some of my favorite ingredients.

Take what you want, leave what you don't. Mix it all up, toss it all out. Taste this, taste that. Be willing to change with the change.

WHAT'S YOUR RECIPE?

If you ask my family, I was a sealed vault. John Dillinger himself couldn't figure out a way to pick my lock.

For whatever reason I wasn't very vocal in expressing the way that I felt or what I needed. Nor was I sure that I needed anything. For years I would always observe my surroundings. Witnessing the way the people around me would walk through life and all that comes with it.

My mother would always offer me a safe space to express how I felt and acknowledge how I internalized everything. It took me down an accidental path of deep examination to learn what worked for me with the understanding that expression of some sorts was my path to liberation.

It started with facing the event that took my father's life. I had an intense curiosity to face the violent events of that Tuesday, September 11, 2001—all the while I knew that I was forcing myself to feel. It was as if I had an instinctual knowledge that I needed to *feel*. And, knowing even at a young age and even to this day how much I internalized. This confrontation was my way of externalizing whether I knew it or not. The result of meeting my trauma head-on led me to externalize my internalization.

I still wasn't able, or wasn't willing, to audibly express what was going on in my mind, body, and soul. I realize now by facing the trauma head-on it led me to a cookbook with a multitude of recipes to try.

I found that my form of expression was writing. I never considered myself a writer but the words seemed to come out easier on paper than they did to say them. But I wanted to say them. Like someone who truly loves singing, who wants to share their voice with the world but only sings in the shower when no one is looking. It took me time, trying different things to finally find the confidence in myself and courage to be vulnerable with my sphere before I was able to share my voice with thousands of people. For me it was about testing different things.

My sister and my mother have always been more organized than I was. More in control. More scheduled. They prefer to know what's to come next rather than be surprised. As if the unknown is a threat.

We all went to a family vacation in New Orleans together. I could feel the tension if we wandered and found a restaurant as opposed to knowing we had a reservation at 3 p.m.

My family needs routine and structure but I prefer spontaneity. This isn't me saying my way is better. I'm simply saying this is *my* way.

After everything our family went through, that difference started to make more sense. Control, I realized, can be a response to chaos. It's not up to me to pinpoint September 11 as being the complete cause of this as much as maybe nature versus nurture. But, when something takes everything from you without asking, routine and a sense of control is a way to feel safe.

I didn't choose that path.

While they needed to know what's coming next I decided to dive into the unknown. I didn't make a decision for what I wanted to do with the rest of my life. I'd say yes to things without doing a deep dive on the consequences. I avoided control like it was the control that's dangerous.

From the outside, it looked like I had no plan. But not having a plan was my plan. When I noticed that life blows up in your face regardless of plans then what's the point of being so rigid? It's not to say plans are bad. I find the strict nature of not being malleable to the way life shakes up your plans is the true danger.

I felt I had more control in accepting a lack of control. A controlled chaos. I found a trusting of myself to respond to the unplanned aspects of life. What could have been labeled as escapism was, for me, a way to survive long enough to eventually get organized on my own terms.

It's a disorganized organized unplanned plan. Chaotic by nature. Though I have no idea if this was the "best" method, it's the choice I made. I had to go through the bad plans to find the good plan and slowly find organization in my life. Constantly, I was criticized by people outside my family that I was too all over the place, wore too many hats, and needed to figure out what I wanted to do for the rest of my life. Turns out, in the current trajectory of humans, it seems better to wear many hats rather than just one, let alone wear a hat that makes me miserable because I decided before I knew what I wanted.

As I write this, I see the tranquility in the veiled security blanket of organization. What was optically moving in the opposite direction of organization and conformity taught me the contrast of how it worked at the same time. Now I seek a bit more structure in my life because I went through that phase. And, honestly, I still am that same guy because I find freestyling life more appealing at times. Continuing the theme of being disorganized, let's go backwards in time to my grief evolution during the immediate youthful years after my father's death.

While I still couldn't express myself through discernible words I'd turned to paper. After learning that the words on paper were simply expressions without sound I learned I could turn these words into noise. That noise became my path to healing. Often, this would primarily be humor, which was stigmatized by a defense mechanism. As I grew up I realized that wasn't the entire truth. Turns out the best defense is offense.

My banter comes from real darkness not as a deflection but as a form of disarmament—a way of simplifying the atrocities of life and seeing them in a different light. Mixing and matching a variety of modalities and giving each one a taste along the way until I learned what my emotional and spiritual taste buds responded to. This is my recipe. It doesn't come with a measuring cup. It's throwing in a little salt, tasting it, and throwing in more when needed. You can try mine if you want but the real question is, what's your recipe? If you don't know then the only way to find out is to step outside of your own world.

There's a vast world out there to engage with until you find what works for you. This was my early journey of grief. It wasn't until I started having these beautiful conversations with strangers that I was exposed to even more ways to grieve fully and live life fully.

One of those ways is being a little easier on myself and a lot more curious.

REPLACE CRITICISM WITH CURIOSITY

I receive messages all the time from people—including mediums. More often than not it's an attempt to get on my podcast, and I have to read between the lines to gauge their authenticity. Because, after all, there are scam artists everywhere so my "East Coast Italian street sense so that I trust no one" radar tends to always be on.

One day I received a direct message from a woman who had a private profile on Instagram. She told me she had mediumship abilities but didn't do it for a living. This woman clarified that she was not asking for money as she just felt the overwhelming intuition to tell me something.

She said my father had some words for me: that my greatest gift is my curiosity. I am a seeker and this has been in part this journey of this podcast and its theme. Listening to an eclectic plate of backgrounds, beliefs, and experiences. I've always felt as if I've been a curious person. Interested in so many different things with a desire to chase every feeling.

My interpretation is perhaps I'm searching for my dad in some subconscious manner. I've always hung my head on not having an experience that was a no-brainer, like maybe I'd get a ghost fart that smelt like broccoli rabe. She said if he did come to me in an undeniable fashion that I would stop seeking.

I've never heard from this woman again. True to her word she never sought anything from me nor did I get even a response back after I messaged in return. A little bit strange but so it goes.

What I'm saying is curiosity is a helpful tool on this journey. Seeking not out of desperation but raw curiosity. There's so much out there in this world that we won't know what is meant for us until we expose ourselves with an interested mind. I find the most joy in this because I've discovered healing mechanisms and perspectives I never would have found if I stood idle.

In tune with curiosity is to lighten up on self-criticism. I think there's a difference between healthy examination and toxic criticism when you're just simply trashing yourself. That does no good. If you catch yourself criticizing yourself, consider a reframe. Instead of a negative connotation flip the judgment into a curious inquiry.

If you think, *Why am I so irritable with others all the time?* Exchange it with something like *What are these feelings of irritability telling me?*

I was told by an old associate of mine that I was my own worst enemy. And they weren't wrong because I am often so hard on myself. And I know this applies to a lot of us. When you catch yourself being too hard on yourself just sprinkle some grace on top of your plate.

There are times for tough love, times to be easy on yourself, and times to be curious with everything. This quest of inquisitiveness leads me to gallop into the unknown. To embrace the unknown, we also need to embrace the fear that tags along. As if we were the Ferdinand Magellan of grief and life. Only this Strait of Magellan is never straight. Grief isn't a straight line. It's a chaotic sketch—sometimes beautiful, sometimes a mess. But we keep drawing anyway.

Staying curiously engaging with life opens existence to limitless possibilities. And, it's not always the happy possibilities. It's in the turmoil of life where our liberation lies. At this point of my life I see suffering as an opportunity.

Oh, life. You sneaky son of a bitch what are you trying to show me this time?

Life keeps handing us tragedies like it's a clearance sale, and we can keep digging through the rack hoping to find the gold. The miracle is, sometimes we find some—and often when we've stopped looking.

SEVERING TIES

There's a forced severing when someone in our life dies. We don't have a choice but to cut ties with the physical person who is no longer touchable. It's hard to grasp because we didn't just lose that person. We now find ourselves embracing those micro-losses. It's a jolt to the nervous system having to adapt to this new normal.

One time I was back in New Jersey visiting my family and I was helping my mom go through old documents that she's held on to. Documents that held memories of the past and all that she had to navigate when her husband died. I saw financial documents, my father's death certificate for the first time, and correspondences with bureaucrats regarding the logistics of the 9/11 aftermath. I had flashes of what my mom did behind the scenes that she never anticipated having to do.

My mother was a hard-working woman who cleaned houses (often with me tagging along since we didn't have a babysitter), sold peanuts at malls, had her own balloon business, all the way to working at a local high school in the administrative department. My father had handled a lot of the financial aspects of the family. My mother now had to jump in, organize, make big decisions without her confidant by her side. All things she maneuvered with such grace and vigor while supporting her grieving children let alone her grieving self.

She was thrust into a new timeline. A new dimension. A reality in which all her daily habits and routines would be altered forever. A forced severing of the way things were into the way things are to be. Though this severing was forced, witnessing all that my mother held manifested from a papyrus time capsule, there can be voluntary severing that helps us on our journey.

There are cultures around the world, including many Indigenous tribes, that have symbolic traditions for grief, transformation, and severing ties with the deceased loved one.

Severing ties sounds insensitive and graphic. My interpretation is not a severing of their memory, legacy, what they meant to us, or even from the pain of grief that comes. I see it as an acceptance of this physical separation. A voluntary action that doesn't represent forgetting, or lack of caring, but a way to move forward without the tangibility of a life gone. An honorable acknowledgment of this new world we just entered without them.

Native American cultures, like the Lakota, would cut their hair when someone in their tribe died. It represented the physical manifestation of the pain and reminder of that physical loss.

In many Indigenous cultures long hair has a powerful significance. It has a spiritual and earthly implication representing spiritual growth. So, to cut it off can represent the time passed with the deceased. The act has a powerful meaning as it relates to the healing process of moving forward without our loved ones yet at the same time keeping them with us. And, to not forget the importance of how physical rituals can be an important aspect of healing.

"In order to understand what is missing, what is gone, you have to understand what it was you had,"[1] explained American psychologist Mary-Frances O'Connor when we discussed the way grief can affect our bodies. We don't have to cut our hair to symbolize our pain, our past, and our steps into this new reality. But it is something to reflect on what hair has

[1] *DEAD Talks*, Episode 196. https://podcasts.apple.com/us/podcast/the-science-of-grief-how-the-brain-body-process-loss-196/id1498553334?i=1000692975250.

represented to Indigenous cultures. If you still have your loved one (or hair in this sense), be present with now before the time comes when they're not there.

Mary also went deeper on these Indigenous rituals. Whenever you get a haircut no one yells and says, "Why isn't your hair growing faster?" It takes time for it to come back at its own natural pace. This regrowing of the hair that was cut takes time and it is a passage of growth. Of new beginnings. Whether you want the new beginning or not, it's out of our control.

This is a physical, emotional, and spiritual process that is a reminder of the life we still have to live and how we can live it while we're still alive in honor of our seemingly bad haircut.

It's not severing ties from the people we lost in a manner of moving on. It's a manner of remembrance and growth. An honoring. A moving into a new phase of life with the emotions of living and grieving.

Although, our loved ones aren't with us anymore their legacy is forever with us and running through us beyond space and time. The sooner we realize this evolvement is a full-body, full-mind, and full-spirit experience (regardless of your beliefs), the more we can move forward as we have more life to live.

Facing this new normal head-on, facing the raw feelings internally and externally with the nod to a future that can represent growth and new beginnings, knowing that even those parts of our hair are chopped off—we still have the roots intact that represent the time we had and the time we still have.

I'm not here to tell you that your new life is going to fill the void or the hole our loved ones left dug with us. It's more an understanding that the shovel is still there for us to dig a new hole. To fill it with whatever we want and to dig as deep as we want. It's a digging that comes with exhaustion and a battle because life is a battle. Even as we fight and duck for cover in the trenches of life, let's remember that our old self may have died, that we're still not dead yet.

As my mother said to me, "This is a battle. Just living life here is a battle. But it's all how you live it. To survive the battle, get beyond the battle, and find that peace."

And, when the fighting quiets and our shovel finally drops, maybe that's when we find out what all this digging really was for.

CHAPTER ELEVEN

WHEN WE DIE

"There's something way more powerful than here."
—My mother, Episode 110

Dr. Mary Helen Hensley recounts being instantly ejected from her body after a near-deadly car accident, observing the scene below with "detached interest" in what was now an out-of-body experience. She describes entering a space where "the music of the spheres" enveloped her, accompanied by a sense of timelessness, as she experienced all her life events simultaneously.

"My concept of linear time literally implodes in my face in that moment . . . . The life is all happening around me simultaneously. So, it's not like it's a beginning, a middle, and an end. It's always happening." Mary tells me how she saw herself at 4 years old, then she looks in another direction where she's 11 years old getting her first bulldog. Dr. Hensley was seemingly able to see various memories from her life simultaneously. Real memories.

She describes this experience as a type of *life review*. A life review is one of the many common themes of near-death experiences (NDEs) I've heard numerous times. Paraphrasing my understanding of its spiritual mechanics is like replaying an old home video without the human ego there to judge—it's been explained to me that it's not from your current "human perspective." You feel every moment, good or bad, from the eyes and hearts of everyone you've ever touched.

She came to the profound realization of time's nonlinearity, where all events of her life occurred at the same time. Observing pivotal moments—both joyful and painful—while understanding how small actions had profound ripple effects. The 72 cents all over again.

Unlike the judgment often depicted in traditional narratives, she found herself evaluating her own life with deep compassion, completely detached from the objective, subjective, and biased outlooks that usually come with this human experience.

This moment of self-judgment contradicted with her religious indoctrination—her father was a Southern Baptist minister who taught that God will judge us in the end. This introspection led her to a paradigm destruction: we are creators of our reality, and life is a web of choices and lessons. She left this experience with an understanding of purpose and an awareness of the eternal connection between all of us.

Her realization that "we chose everything we are experiencing here today" transformed her understanding of life and death. She recalls meeting her "guardians," who reminded her that they have been and are always with her, guiding her. Perhaps, that guiding can come in the form of our little internal voice, intuition, gut feelings, or in the synchronicities in everyday life. That we are "fractals of the same whole" and architects of our own reality—which reframed her entire existence.[1]

[1] *DEAD Talks*, Episode 178. https://podcasts.apple.com/us/podcast/near-death-experience-spiritual-guides-life-choices/id1498553334?i=1000672992031.

BYE-BYE CANCER

"When I died, I had stage two cancer. When I came back, it was gone."

—Rosemary Ringer

Not long after Rosemary Ringer was discharged from the hospital following a biopsy procedure for her stage two cancer she realized something was wrong. At home, she began hemorrhaging heavily after a surgical error, which led to her clinical death.

She expressed how she was in a dark place leading to her near-death for quite some time after her husband committed suicide in the same home where she was bleeding out. She stood in the shower contemplating whether to call for help or just let death take her away. Fortunately, she called for help which got her to the emergency room, where her blood pressure dropped to fatal levels and which was the moment she felt catapulted out of her body.

Slowly she felt herself floating away into what she described as a black void. She knew immediately that she had died saying, "Everything I really am went with me."

Rosemary then sensed a spiritual pretense on her left, which introduced itself as "the Original." This being affirmed her identity as being created in God's image.

She was very familiar with the Bible having read it multiple times. She had never aligned with traditional biblical teachings, considering herself a slight heretic for having used her own free will to form her own opinions.

The spiritual presence felt warm and filled with love as they welcomed her home. Then she was engulfed in a mist of light particles that cleansed her of the earthly "muck," as she put it, which included her grief, guilt, and pain.

"These are not droplets of vapor. They're particles of light, and you're being cleansed of the muck of earth." Then suddenly she was standing before a door that represented the transition to the next realm. She was told that going through that door wasn't the divine will for her life. As if it was a spiritual spark note that she wasn't supposed to officially die—it wasn't part of her story. It wasn't part of the life she chose. Even with that friendly disclosure it was made clear to her that she had a choice to walk through the door or to come back. Another choice.

And boy did she come back. Right before she died, she saw a vision of a nurse grieving deeply over her death. As if she felt everything that nurse was feeling with such deep empathy that the word *empathy* doesn't even seem enough to express the depth of which she felt.

She thought, "If I can spare one person that much pain, I have to go back."

She chose to return to spare the nurse of this emotion and like a flick of a light switch found herself back in her body. She was conscious and found with no lasting physical or cognitive damage to boot.

Rosemary was clinically dead for over 10 minutes. And, after this event they later found that her cancer had completely evaporated. The doctors had no explanation. Some may say this was just an intense dream and doubt her healing. She doesn't seem to care who believes her because she tells me she's healed.

And also will someone else please tell me the last time they had a dream like this?[2]

SPIRITUALITY OVER RELIGION

> *"I don't disrespect religion, but I've been there, and I know the truth of the other side."*
>
> —Philip Siracusa

[2] *DEAD Talks*, Episode 158. https://podcasts.apple.com/us/podcast/she-died-saw-the-afterlife-and-came-back-healed-158/id1498553334?i=1000656868164.

Philip Siracusa was 14 years old when he had what he calls a NDE. In 1981, he went in for a routine dental procedure. He was given *sweet air* (nitrous oxide but this sounds more fun). Due to an allergy, he was unaware that his body began to shut down, which caused him to stop breathing.

As we've heard before, he described the feeling of levitating out of his body where he could actually see himself, his mother, and the dentist.

"I was waving, saying, 'Hello, can you hear me?' but no one responded."

He was then pulled through a dark tunnel at an unimaginable speed. Even within this utter darkness he didn't feel any fear or pain. Off in the distance he noticed a pinhole of light slowly starting to appear, which then expanded into an immense vibrant sky. "It was the most beautiful sky, beyond any words I could use to describe it."

Philip found himself in a garden where everything was perfect. More perfect than perfect. The flowers, the trees, and the grass. "Every blade of grass was alive and vibrating with energy." He told me that the other side was "more real than here." That this new world he found himself in made our reality feel as if it were just an illusion. A veil covering the truth of our endless origin.

He had a sister who died at birth. And, on the "other side" he met a girl whom he believed was his sister on a park bench. She said to follow her; he knew he was completely safe with her. Though, he couldn't be certain it was his sister he believes it was her. As if a knowingness that it was someone he should know and belong with.

He saw his grandparents, including his grandfather, whom he'd never met, "He looked so vibrant, in his sixties but not aged like we think of here." Then Philip got a message from his grandmother who told him to go back.

Philip then felt a pull backwards. A force pulling him through the tunnel in which he arrived for the great return into his human body.

Although he was raised Catholic, he now doesn't follow any religion after coming back with knowledge he believed to be true and that has completely altered the way he sees our existence and thereafter. He came back with the understanding that we choose what we want to experience in this life which he defined as a *soul contract*. Just another theme that I've heard time and again from those who've had NDEs.

The love on the other side, as he commented, is unconditional. It's even more powerful than the love we can comprehend here. Everything there is connected through love and energy. He now sees religion just as one of many frameworks humans use to explain the divine. He views God as a universal energy or vibration rather than a personal deity tied to any specific religious concepts.

To me even though billions of people refer to a God in their own way—through different stories or attachments—maybe we're believing in the same thing just in different ways.

He closed by saying, "Believe only what you believe for your reality because you are the creator of your existence."

MY MOM

> *"It's almost like you close your eyes, but you're dreaming it, but you're really there. You weren't in a body, and I just remember looking—I didn't even have to look down and look around. I knew I wasn't in my body."*

We were told my mother was awake. She was conscious for the first time since her cardiac arrest. I'll never forget our first hug; she seemingly recognized who I was through the foggy transition back. It was clear she wasn't herself just yet after such a traumatic bodily experience on top of all the sedation. But she was awake. And she knew I was her son.

It was too soon to tell if she'd have any long-term damage and for now we were grateful her heart was still beating. Though she seemed different, she was sitting up confidently. She acted as if she had pep in her step with a supernatural giddiness. Seemingly herself in her purest form.

At this point my mom can't even gather what she's doing in the hospital.

After some moments go by of collecting ourselves and embracing the moment, it's what she said next that I'll never forget.

She asked where her father was.

My sisters and Ken (my mother's partner) all looked at each other surprised and perplexed. My Grandpa John, her father, died in 1988 before I was born.

With Neapolitan persistence my mom looked at us like we were idiots when we questioned her. She asserted that her father was here in the hospital and that's why she was here. She was unable to comprehend that she was in a hospital gown hooked up to an IV and monitors.

We had to constantly remind her (like Dory from *Finding Nemo*) what had happened because her short-term memory was shot. Which was scary at first. It was at that moment that I knew she may have just had an experience. My mom must have seen her father.

If I hadn't gone down this path of having these NDE conversations with some of my podcast guests, I would have instinctually interpreted her response as psychosis and trauma.

She hadn't recollected any spiritual experience at this point. I didn't doubt her; I didn't try to tell her she didn't just see him. But we had to find a calming way of telling her that Grandpa John wasn't here and we were in the hospital for her. Because she wasn't willing to just accept that he wasn't here even when the nurse told her he wasn't.

I had to get the nurse to come in to gently let her know that there was no John Romano in the hospital. My mother said that there's no way, *she just saw him*. She tried to even stand up and go find out for herself, which was a delight to see her beautiful fire reignite.

After preventing her from getting up, I remember kneeling down next to her. None of us knew what the best approach was. Do we play along? Instead, we chose to slowly recount the timeline of her life rather just yell like a desensitized lunatic that he's been dead for 35 years.

"Mom, Grandpa John isn't here."

I broke down the year I was born and that I never met Grandpa John. We'd slowly bring up her past of being in Brooklyn at the hospital for her father and she'd slowly recollect memories.

Step-by-step, memory by memory she'd have flashes that her father did die. Then came the heartbreaking moment etched in my heart. She broke down in tears as if she just learned her father died for the first time.

It was a seesaw of remembering and forgetting dwelling on the fact that her father wasn't there.

Little by little she would recollect the day he died and the funeral. Then revert to a depth of tears that only a daughter would express learning she just lost her father. I contemplated that what she experienced during her NDE must have felt so real that she felt she was literally just with him. Mixed with whatever chemicals are coursing through her veins and the overall trauma of her heart stopping.

This seesaw went on for a week and then the same thing happened when she recalled her mother. Then my sister Jacqueline turned to me and asked if our mother thought our dad was still alive. When that conversation eventually happened, it was just me and my mother in the hospital room.

I woke up a couple of mornings later after virtually no sleep in a damn recliner that wouldn't recline. That's when my mom asked, "Where's Dave?"

I tilted my head in confusion asking, "Dave? You mean me?"

She goes, *"No . . . Dad!,"* as if I'm losing my mind.

Here we go again. She doesn't remember that my dad died, and my heart sunk in preparation for the worst déjà vu.

Similarly to the experience with her father I believed again, *Oh, she saw my dad.* I took a similar approach step-by-step asking if she remembered where my father worked. She instantly remembered he worked in the World Trade Center. I then followed up asking if she remembered what had happened there. Assisting her in the remembering piece by piece to see if she could put it together.

As if returning from an alternative universe she exclaimed that of course she remembers 9/11 but "he got out." I took a breath and told her that he didn't. And, for the second time I had to watch my mom grieve all over again like she found out for the very first time.

My throat constricted and my eyes welled up, because I wanted to somehow bottle up her pain and take it from her.

I found peace in a knowingness that she saw my father, but without confirmation just yet that my father may have come to her while she was under. I believe it was the next day after this grueling experience I went home so I could go shower and sleep for a couple hours and my sisters took over.

Around noon that day I then got a text from my sister saying, "Mom remembers seeing Daddy!"

I was so excited to hear it. Exactly what we all thought was coming came. As my mother slowly started clearing up she could remember feeling my father's presence during her NDE.

Within minutes of my sister's text I received a message from a medium named Amber whom I had on my show.

She messaged me sending me *love and light* knowing that my mother was in the hospital. Amber didn't pry. Now looking back, she seemed to be waiting for my permission to tell me what she told me next.

I told her how strange I felt it was that she, a medium, reached out at the exact moment my sister told me my mother remembers seeing my father.

Amber then sent me the following message that rocked my world:

> That's crazy 'cause your dad just bugged me and said 'can you tell her the thing she needs to take care of is herself. She's not very good at it and is always worried about everyone else. She's been given the gift of time to learn how to love herself just as much as she loves other people.' And he said even though he loves her, he doesn't want her to join him anytime soon. And he wants you to say those words to her. Exactly like he said them.

Skeptics may think these words are too general. But they're not. My sisters and I had conversations about if/when my mother comes out of this that it'll shift a few things. She's always caring about other people and always puts herself second. My mother takes care of herself physically more than anyone I know but I've always had the feeling that she could do a better job focusing on herself spiritually and emotionally. We'd hope she'd take care of herself more and release the weight of worry for others.

The alignment of this message from Amber as she says is from my dad was spot-on, let alone the fact that my mother confirmed that my father told her multiple times that she needs to *go back* and that she's not supposed to be here.

The timing of the message from Amber blows my mind. To me it's hard to deny this. This perhaps isn't tangible evidence. It's experiential but I think that's all we have. And maybe the proof is in the feeling. These experiences that we must have personally to truly understand the magnitude.

To add to this profound experience, weeks later when my mother came home, she had a spontaneous and more vivid remembrance of what she experienced.

She recalled seeing not only my father but also her parents and her brother. As she sketched on a napkin the landscape she was surrounded by them. My dad to the left, then her brother Tommy, then her parents. She felt a presence behind her parents that came in the form of two but couldn't distinguish who they were but she felt them. And she felt like she was *home.*

And maybe that's what it is. Maybe it's just going *home.* A place where we were before and where we'll be after this temporary journey. A home that is like no other. A home where everything makes sense. *Worry* isn't in the dictionary of this spiritual plane. Perhaps it's just incomprehensible to most of our levels of sensory perception.

On one of our podcasts together she explained, "I felt like I belonged there. This is where I was supposed to be . . . . I felt such a connection of oneness."

My mother said within this oneness there weren't faces or bodies. But she could feel and understand who they were. Just a knowing. Spiritual embodiments if you will. She was at peace; she was happy and giddy aligned with the same vibe I felt when she was in the hospital bed. A tethered transition between two realms.

She doesn't know what this experience was. She didn't bring up God or Jesus. She doesn't tie it to religion. She just had an experience without definition yet a yearning for understanding why.

This experience was real to her. Because it was real.

My mom came out of it confused about what she experienced, but it's also brought her peace—now with a different grasp on what's potentially next. It's a level of peace that all will be okay and the loved ones that we often say we lost are merely just waiting for us.

It altered her reality, and it certainly has affected mine. You'd think I'd be more prepared for these experiences, but it's when these things happen to you that you realize preparation certainly helps but there just isn't a substitution for experience.

All the stories I've heard told are further separated from my life. They're quite impactful when you hear them in droves but it's different when it happens to someone so close in your life. A truly undeniable source.

THE BLACK

But what about the black?

For every person who sees something profound when they "died," there are others who see absolutely nothing. I get messages every week from people saying, "My heart stopped, I died, and there was just darkness."

I've seen this lead people to believe there is no afterlife. And, honestly, if you *only* go by that experience, I understand why. It's an argument that NDEs could be nothing more than the brain's final fireworks show.

Maybe there's nothing. It's all just a cosmic accident with no depth of purpose where a great big bang came out of nowhere just so we can sit through terrible reality TV shows.

Maybe it is neurological. Maybe it is dimethyltryptamine flooding the brain. It's just as possible as anything else. But isn't it fascinating that our brains can even do this at all? We just chalk it up to imagination and brain trickery when these experiences *feel* real. It makes me question what real really is.

Why do some people have profound experiences and some don't?

I heard a theory that stuck with me—not as truth, but as a "huh . . . maybe."

It goes like this. "Old souls" experience more vivid NDEs because they've done this before. Their soul recognizes the light, the love, the pull, God, or whatever you want to call it—and knows it isn't their time. It's why so many say they were given a choice to return. While younger souls, less experienced if you will, might be overwhelmed by that unconditional love and not want to go back, even though they're not "supposed" to stay. Like a fly seeing the light of an electric buzz trap completely unable to stop flying to the light because it doesn't know any better.

If they touched the incomprehensible love on the other side, they simply wouldn't come back so they were shown nothing.

Ten years ago, I would've rolled my eyes and asked for a hit of whatever weed inspired that theory. Now, I'm not so quick to dismiss. My mind is more open than a 24-hour fitness. Some of this makes zero sense. Some of it makes complete sense. That's the beauty of it.

Take Blake Kasemeier—former guest and an atheist (at the time of recording): "When someone is gone, they are gone. . . . I am an atheist. And no disrespect to anybody who has faith in God or the afterlife, et cetera, but that's just my personal belief."

He goes on to compare it to Occam's razor, which is a problem-solving principle that suggests the most likely explanation for something is probably the simplest one.

I can understand why someone would need substantial evidence to believe. The most common answer I've come across as to why someone doesn't believe in anything happening when we pass is due to logical, more objective thinking. To me and what I've been exposed to it seems more likely that we do continue on in some fashion. Yet, I can't *prove it* in the court of existential law—at the same time I haven't seen proof from an atheist either.

"And, despite a lot of people finding this belief system sad I don't always see it like that." Blake continues, "With being an atheist, I feel responsible for carrying whatever that world was that we made."

He incidentally leverages his beliefs to feel some sort of responsibility to carry on his mother's legacy. Back to the idea that this life is all we get he wants to make the most of it for himself and continue his mother's existence through his living and storytelling. This is his basis of legacy with a unique perspective as to why it's important to him. It's beautiful if you ask me.

This just leads me to continue my own processing of a completely different belief system that regardless of our beliefs life and death ultimately come down to the meaning we give it. There are a lot of thoughts, beliefs, theories, unique experiences, and ideas out there in the world.

Although, the emo side of me thinks that just blackness kind of sounds like a relief. As positive as I like to keep it and how beautiful life is, sometimes I just exhale and think that maybe eternal unawareness into nothingness is a nice reprieve. Because after all, we won't even be aware so what would it matter.

I've instinctually found the idea of nothingness less inspiring while the atheists I've connected with have found it more inspiring. We truly only have one shot at this life so while we're here we might as well make the best of it. I've seen this notion offer more meaning to some. However, the more I contemplate eternal nothingness the more I can't stand it. I don't like the idea of it; it bothers me and makes me feel icky.

Even with my own convictions I don't dismiss the idea of *nothingness.* I want to hear about every ideology out there. I want to collect the data and expose myself to ideas I've never imagined without immediately dismissing them. Perhaps this exposure can open our minds and help us develop our own reverie to be a moth to our own flame.

Maybe with the thousands of religions in the world there is some universal origin of truth buried.

Just maybe.

10,000

Christianity says souls are judged by God. You get an all-access pass to heaven if you're righteous, hell even if you're not, and maybe a pit stop in purgatory, as if you're in spiritual TSA.

Islam also centers judgment. Souls are weighed by Allah, and you get paradise or punishment depending on how you lived.

Hinduism, Buddhism, Sikhism, and Jainism lean more into cycles: birth, death, rebirth. Names change—Moksha, Nirvana, union with

Waheguru—but the basic idea is the same: we keep coming back until we unhook from the Ferris wheel.

Judaism has a range of views, and I've read a lot revolving around "the world to come": a perfect reality after the Messiah, with its own flavor of judgment and restoration.

Atheism. I could say *nothing* about that but it's when you're gone, you're gone. No heaven, no hell, no cosmic Google review—just lights out, buddy. And I've seen this belief motivate as much as any religious framework. If this is all there is, then make it count.

Then there's the newer kids on the block—like Scientology, started in the 1950s by L. Ron Hubbard, a man who literally holds the Guinness World Record for most published works of science fiction. There are millions of people who follow this path, which is interesting to consider. If Dr. Seuss started a religion, we might be tithing in the Green Eggs and Ham afterlife.

There are roughly 10,000 religions in the world, so if I missed yours, don't come at me in the comments. The point is: there are thousands of maps and one mysterious territory. The more I learn, the less I know—and somehow, the less I know, the more I'm convinced there is something. At the end of death (day), I think it's whatever helps you live and love while you're here. It's personal. It's yours.

I've always felt the desire to question. And it's not for sport, to be a dick, or to diminish others' beliefs. It's to learn. There's a big old world out there, let alone universe, and I've continually sought what resonates with me—pulling from different ideologies that I've consolidated on my own. To be malleable in my beliefs because there's always more to uncover and not be afraid to change paths.

I get excited to explore feeling like I may never find an answer, but I can certainly find some comfort. And I can certainly go cross-eyed. Perhaps the answers I may or may not get are just in the seeking. That this life is about seeking.

WHAT I BELIEVE

> *"Know that to depart from this mortal world is to be born into a world that is everlasting, to leave this lowly dust for a kingdom that is celestial, to exchange affliction and sorrow for a state of complete joy and gladness."*

I've gone down the rabbit hole digging into religious and spiritual explanations of the afterlife, pairing them with hundreds of conversations I've had through *DEAD Talks*. That's when I stumbled onto the Bahá'í Faith. I knew nothing about it, and still really don't, but reading a simple summary made me think, *Holy shit—this is basically what I've come to believe,* without ever knowing this religion existed. So, if the Bahá'ís are into some weird shit, please don't assume this is a co-sign.

The Bahá'í Faith frames the afterlife as a spiritual realm where the soul moves closer to—or further from—God, "source," depending on earthly actions and spiritual development. To me, this resonates deeply. It suggests that life is a revolving door of lessons intertwined with our spiritual advancement.

This struck me. Not because I suddenly proclaim this as adherence to this faith, but because it matched the shape of what I've slowly pieced together. Representing my eclectic gatherings from various vantage points each with a grain of salt. Simply stated: that life isn't a one-and-done event—it's a series of lessons, and a checkpoint in a continuation of learning.

Maybe religions come from the same origin. They may be seemingly contradictory by nature but if we look deep enough, there are some similar themes in different jackets. From that divine origin the foundation of spiritual progress was birthed and spread like branches from a tree in different directions. Abraham taught faith, Moses taught structure, Jesus taught love, Muhammed taught justice. Different branches, maybe one root.

And, over thousands of years, through human interpretation, trauma, ego, kings, politics, and bad translations, the roots got distorted. Diluted. But the core feels similar: grow, serve, learn, love, evolve.

Most people I've ever met—religious, spiritual, atheist, chaotically neutral—are all trying to grow. To become better. To heal. To understand. If the soul is real, maybe earth is the gritty part of the curriculum. The remedial class. The lab portion where emotions are sharpened and consequences hurt, and grief punches you in the gut until you pay attention.

Science matters, too. So can religion. So does institution. Honestly, I'm doing what I'm sure some of you are doing: stealing pieces from everywhere and building my own belief system like legal plagiarism.

My belief about the afterlife is simple—I believe we continue on. To unpack that, I'm not sure we can get this life wrong. I understand how that sounds because there is incredible evil in this world and from our earthly understanding it can be black and white. But it leads me to wonder if evil and tragedy exists for our spiritual advancement.

I am not a religious man by societal definition. I don't adhere to the Bible as I was taught from my little upbringing. A lot of my mass comes with a lot of side-eye thinking its foundation is based on control and limiting the consciousness of the masses. But let's not throw the baby out with the bathwater.

I enjoy learning about as many perspectives and religious contexts as possible to seek my truth. I mostly relish in learning through experience. But I value learning about various perspectives, seeking consistencies that hint at various theories or beliefs: that all religions may stem from a single source, dispersed over time and culture, shaped by histories we can't trace. All the while juggling the foundation that religion has been used as a major source of control. And concurrently with that shadow I don't dismiss the good that comes from it.

Take Genesis 11:6, "The Lord said, 'If as one people speaking the same language, they have begun to do this, then nothing they plan to do will be impossible for them.'"

This reference to the Tower of Babel aligns with the necessity of challenges in life—growth requires friction.

Could reincarnation be part of this growth? Stories of past-life regression and NDEs suggest it. Life might be a choice—one we revisit until we gravitate closer to the source. And sometimes I wonder if my father's death was sewn into whatever plan my soul signed up for. Maybe he passed the soulful baton on purpose—because losing him became the very reason I speak, write, and attempt to guide others now. I don't pretend to know how that works for the many others who died that day. But I do believe it led somewhere for each of them.

The only doubt I have about the afterlife stems from the obvious one in that *I don't know for sure*. And weirdly, the uncertainty is comforting now. It makes faith feel like a choice instead of a requirement. I don't believe we live, die, then rot into worm food and that's it. And if I'm wrong, I'll be too dead to be embarrassed.

What really gives me a warm feeling in my belly is how magical life already is. The fact that billons of us each live inside our own private reality. That emotions hurt more than broken bones. That I can feel something is off when I walk into a room without seeing anything through that gut feeling. That invisible frequencies carry voices across the world, and we just shrug it off as routine.

And then there's the cosmos that remind me with an inverted neck that we're floating on a rock held down by the invisible force of gravity. We're blanketed by immeasurable glowing balls of hydrogen gas we call stars heated by a fire ball that can fit 1.3 billion earths in it. Sure. Just an accident. Nothing to see here.

As comedian Pete Holmes put it best: "If nothing sometimes spontaneously erupts into everything, that's a pretty goddamn magical nothing."

Pete's argument is not only witty but depicts a simple profoundness. If nothingness can't exist, and science can't prove God, then whether you believe in a creator or not, you're left with something intangible. His conclusion: "If your nothingness is magical, that's heaven, bitch!"

He goes on to say that those who believe in "nothing" also believe God doesn't exist. He counters by saying, "You know what doesn't exist? Nothing."

The defining character of nothingness is indeed that it doesn't exist. That leaves us with an option that a God does exist but is something you can't see, touch, taste, or photograph, and that science can't prove. Or you think it's just nothing—something you can't see, touch, taste, photograph, and that science can't prove.

For me, it sounds even more far-fetched to think this existence is for naught. How could life—a weird, emotional, faux material experience—serve no purpose? Then again, maybe. But I'll invest my existential dollar on the former.

Many of us, including myself in my early life, say that *no one knows.* And I get why that's a common thing to say because on the surface level it seems *no one knows.* At this point in my life, I'm not so quick to say that.

I understand why—it's easy to accept on the surface. Yet mediums, those who experience NDEs, and even my own mother, have shared stories that suggest otherwise. While anecdotal, these accounts—thousands of them, with parallels running rampant—are hard to ignore.

Of course, some NDE stories and mediums are exploitative. Not all are doing it from good or can be considered legit. Just like every aspect of life there are scammers. And that is an area of diligence that should not be taken lightly. I've had experiences with mediums when nothing resonated and I felt this person was just full of shit. You can find these people in every area of life.

Again, perhaps we're just not equipped to comprehend what's next. Yet.

I cannot merely neglect the possibility that nothing happens. I cannot affirm anything that I've said is so. As a short simple answer to contradict my notion of my belief not being absolute—there's no way this is it.

The feeling I get in the core of me, the stories I hear, the experiences I have are too powerful. And it makes more sense that *something* continues rather than *nothing*.

If you need hard proof, I can't give you that. I haven't found it either. I don't believe the same proof is in the cards to date. I can't give you a shrunken glove to put on to determine if your belief fits or not. If science is our liberation to this burden of proof, then science just has to catch up. For anyone that relies on proof, can you prove to me that there isn't an afterlife? I'll wait . . .

Live and let live. The more I partner experience with seeking, the more I learn that there is so much more out there and I exponentially know less.

We may never truly know what happens when we die. But the way we live, the stories we pass on, and the connections we make—those echoes might be the closest thing to eternity that we can understand from this side.

Four words I think we'd all be better off saying more often are '*I do not know*.' I am so deeply rooted in the belief that some things are beyond comprehension, for now, that it's become a relief instead of a threat.

So, we're left here, together, in faith and the unknown.

For some people, that's terrifying. For me, that's where the living starts. Because if we can accept that we don't fully know things, then we can stop pretending we have to feel safe. We can stop using certainty as armor. We can stop fighting to win the argument and instead ask, *How do I want to live while I'm here?*

I don't know what happens when we die.

I barely know what's going to happen in the next 24 hours.

But I do know this: we're here right now. Right now, in the sweet spot of this precise moment that is eternally fleeting into the next. We get to love. We get to screw up. We get to forgive and be forgiven. We get to tell stories and listen and wonder and cry and laugh and look up at the sky and think, *What the hell is all of this?* And somehow, that wondering feels sacred enough.

The wizardry isn't having the answers.

It's in standing inside the not knowing, and still choosing to live.

Screenshot of an Instagram direct message from psychic medium and former guest Amber Cavanagh sent the morning my mother remembered seeing my father in the hospital.

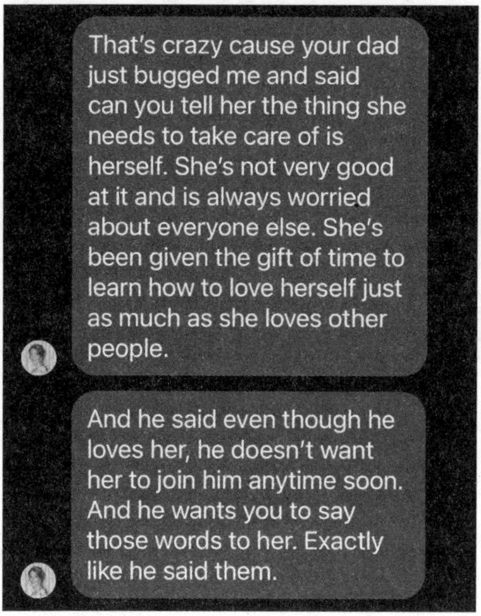

Sketch my mother drew on a napkin immediately after recalling what she saw and felt during her near-death experience. The outer circles represent my father, her brother Tommy, and her parents. The single circle in the center represents where she felt she was.

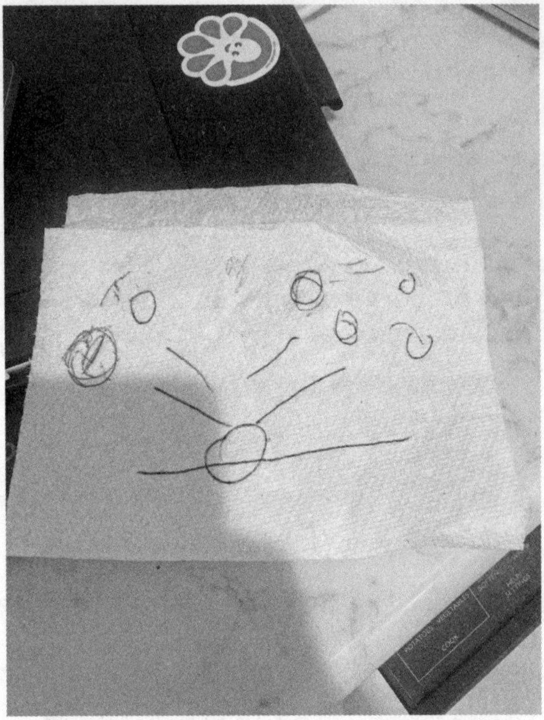

CHAPTER TWELVE

IT'S OKAY TO KNOW NOTHING

"I was filled with all these questions and I had no idea what was going on."

—Max Berlin, Episode 100

September 11, 2001 was a beautiful day. The kind of day that tricks you into believing you understand how life works. The sun rose the way it always does, indifferent and routine. People woke up believing they knew their day. My father knew his alarm would ring. He knew he'd drive to the commuter lot off Exit 117 of the Garden State Parkway. He knew he'd get to work, put in his hours, and come home to us. That was the plan. His plan.

I woke up knowing I'd go to school. I knew I'd count down the minutes to gym class. I knew the bell would ring and I'd walk home with my best friend, hoping the ice cream man made an appearance. I knew that when the sun dipped and the streetlights buzzed on, my dad would walk through the garage door like he always did.

That's not what happened.

And it turned out neither of us knew anything at all.

I'd been to funerals before. My grandpa died when I was young. But that felt . . . allowed. Expected. Old people are supposed to die. Parents aren't. Fathers aren't allowed to die until *they're* old. Mine wasn't. Not yet.

What I didn't understand then, but would come to understand in every way possible, is that life can turn upside down, sideways, and inside out in an instant. You can do everything "right." Plan, prepare, follow the rules, stick to routines, stay organized, pretend you're steering the ship and not know there's an iceberg dead ahead. Something unseen can reach in and rearrange everything that you thought you knew was coming.

It planted a seed in me that would sprout when I was old enough to understand it: the illusion of control is just that—an illusion.

We may try to outthink the uncertainty. To grip harder. To stay ahead of disaster. But the tighter we hold on, the more life can slip through the cracks of our clenched metaphorical fists. Eventually I learned something that felt like both defeat and relief.

Not knowing is not a flaw or unsafe—it's life.

When my mind races, when my body tightens, when my biology hijacks my clarity, that's when I stop myself. I lift my tired neck toward the sky, open my arms just enough to loosen the armor, and say to myself—sometimes whisper, sometimes mutter out loud—"I don't know."

Three terrifying words. Three liberating words. A soft rebellion. A conscious surrender.

The world teaches us that confidence means certainty. But I've learned that confidence is just with ourselves. That certainty is often the thing that traps us and hurts us more when it turns to shit. And, then when things turn to shit to just give it a little more time. It demands we predict what can't be predicted.

Letting go of the need to know what's next, what was supposed to happen, or what "should" have been has opened my life in ways I couldn't have engineered if I tried. We cling to control because we think it creates safety—but the truth is, half of the safety we feel is just the story we tell ourselves.

The need for control of the deepest patterns I've seen in humans—including myself. It's biological. Hardwired for us to scan for danger, to anticipate the future so we can avoid pain. But now, in a world spinning faster than our nervous systems can process, suddenly control becomes anxiety wearing a responsible mask.

Not knowing doesn't make you weak—it makes you human. And full control? It's not real. Presence and what we focus on is real.

Change doesn't ask for permission. It just shows up.

That doesn't mean don't make plans or goals. I'm all for intention, direction, dreams. Just don't marry them for the tax breaks. Hold them softly.

Most of our suffering comes from trying to force life into the version we wrote in our heads. We grieve the gap between expectation and reality. I've reached the point where I'm more shocked when things *do* go the way I planned.

Here's what I've learned: be clear about what you want but be willing to become someone new on the way there. Let the path bend because when someone we love dies, let alone just living life, the path already has bent.

We're not here to know all the answers, and it's okay not to know what to do. Lean into the confidence in yourself even when the next step isn't clear. Even when you have no idea what to do and feel like everything is out of control. Engage with the questions we ask ourselves more than worrying about the answers because it's in the contemplation that may birth some sort of resolution.

It's important to understand that sometimes life is driving through the fog. Where you can't see more than a few feet ahead and it's terrifying not knowing if there's a turn coming or a cliff. All you can do is stay with what's right in front of you and where you focus your thought energy.

Listen for clues. Adapt as the road shifts. Sit in mystery and stop forcing it into clarity.

Because the truth is simple: we do not always control the external, we can control the internal, and we do control how gently we meet the unknown.

And that might be the closest thing to freedom that I've found.

And then there's that one stingy little thing we do know:

We will die.

It sounds like a blunt transition, but it has become one of my greatest teachers about control and not knowing. Death reminds me this is all temporary—pain, joy, discomfort, confusion, love. All of it. Nothing stays. And because it doesn't stay makes it more precious. It pulls me back into the only place I know: the right now.

Health also levels the playing field.

The billionaire.

The monk.

The TSA agent pissed off at your laptop.

The newborn.

We're all headed toward the same exit door.

We don't dictate our ending. We can influence our longevity—eat well, exercise, look both ways when we cross the street, take vitamins—but that's not a bilateral contract. It's an attempt to control with good intentions.

My mother is proof of this. I know very few people in better shape for their age than my mom. She moves her body regularly, eats clean, and her supplement cabinet looks prepped for the GNC apocalypse. She tried to control everything in ways that we're taught to, and her heart still stopped. No warning. No negotiation.

Society led me to expect that I'd have my father my entire life. Death told me otherwise.

This is where the bridge of control and death cross the impermanent river. We think we're steering and create an insurmountable amount of pressure to know how things are going to go and freak out about doing the right things. When we can just let go and trust the unknown.

This is meant to liberate. When we can calibrate this notion, it erases the neurotic hamster wheel of thoughts we get tangled in: timelines, pressures to have it all figured out, to know if we're grieving right. Death removes the illusions that we know what we're doing and that maybe it's not about knowing at all.

If we knew every step, every answer, every outcome—life would be a machine. It can be a choice: the unknown can be the very thing that gives life its magic or we give into the fear.

Death is both known and unknowable. The strangest paradox blending two opposites. The most inevitable thing we do know and yet the biggest uncertainty of all. An ambiguous riddle of our existence.

Impermanence can scare us—or set us free. When we fully embrace that nothing lasts, we start to see now as the only thing that really matters. This exact breath. This exact heartbeat. This moment. It's the only thing we're ever guaranteed.

You don't have to know what your next step is. It could land in mud, on pavement, or in a pile of shit. The point isn't knowing. The point is taking the step despite what we lose, gain, or encounter.

When my father died suddenly none of us had any idea what to do. We had no idea what the rest of our life would look like or how we'd feel in the next hour. We lost control of everything. There's no script for a world that has been punched out of its axis.

Control wasn't just gone—it evaporated. The future we thought we had evaporated with it.

All we can do was focus on the very next step, but the key is to take that step. Step into the unknown and not focus on whether it's the right step. Not the perfect step. Just a step. My family and I moved through those days like we were walking underwater. Each choice a determinedness, each emotion an uneven wave. In grief you just try to breathe through the fear of not knowing if things will even be okay.

The thing about grief is it doesn't just break your heart. It breaks your sense of direction. Your compass points south.

Grief throws you into the depths of the unknown. One day you're living in the familiar, routinely predictable and then the next you're in uncharted territory. Nothing feels certain. Nothing feels safe. Even when your own thoughts feel foreign.

It's the seemingly uncontrollable unknown where we can decide to see not as the enemy but just a new landscape to learn to live in.

The moment I started to understand that control is borrowed and that none of us truly know what we're doing I began to live a life of responding, feeling, adapting, and trying again. Letting go of the results and just taking my best step forward.

You don't have to know the map. You just have to stay in motion.

Grief is the great unmasking. How unpredictable this all is. And how deeply human it is to *feel* lost when you're not lost at all. You're just stepping into the fog.

Maybe that's what living truly is. Learning to drive, walk, crawl through the fog with your hands out and heart open with the willingness to admit—"I don't know."

Because that's the only honest place we can begin.

YOU'RE NOT LOST

After living through the type of loss that erases the ground benefiting you, certainty stopped feeling safe—it felt suffocating. Diving into the unknown became its own kind of rebellion. And, letting go of the worry of where I'll end up.

I graduated college in 2011 and that summer I bartended to make a little extra cash after making the decision to drive to Los Angeles to possibly make it a home. People have asked me why I decided to make this move and the answer really is I don't know. I felt a sideways gravitational pull to *just go*. Just like the feeling of chasing something I haven't identified yet. Essentially, doing the opposite of what my foundational scars have taught me. I would move *further* away from my family and the rocks in my life to chase something I couldn't quite identify. Now looking back, I was chasing life. I was chasing every feeling to see how cold the water felt in the deep end of the unknown.

That October, two of my friends and I decided to jump in my two-door Acura overpacked with the limited items we owned and decided to drive west. We were guaranteed a place to stay for a month with my buddy's angelic sister who was kind enough to house three young men fresh out of college.

I ended up taking the job I interviewed for on Craigslist in which I sold reusable hot and cold packs, frozen cheesecake, and knives at Costco, Albertsons, and Sam's Club. On my days off I'd work at a reputable production company reading scripts and organizing my boss's contact list. I thought I wanted to dabble in the film industry and be as cliché as possible.

We ended up getting our own apartment after overstaying our uncontracted month freebie. We officially moved to Los Angeles. Young men with no plans, no understanding of what we were going to do the entire time. We were figuring it out. We were on an adventure where we couldn't see the forest through the trees but we kept going.

I had job after job just to make do. I lived at times with five guys in a two-bedroom apartment to make rent more affordable. During the years I was there I felt an unspoken whisper from those back east wondering what the heck I was doing. The echoes of worry that David is lost, indecisive, and scattered. Perhaps I was. But to me if something is never lost then how can anything be found? I don't even believe I was ever lost. I believe I was seeking in uncharted territory. And anything new is uncharted territory.

Everything I've done has led me to this moment. And everything I've done preceding this moment is filled with uncertainty, disappointments, achievements, more disappointments, mistakes, existential and emotional crisis. All of which may have been subconsciously guided by the undercurrent of a boy's life turned upside down by the death of his father.

I'd have to write another book for my Los Angeles adventures. This first leap moving away from all that I loved set the tone for the rest of my life.

In 2016, I did exactly that. I was reeling from my first real romantic heartbreak. The relationship unraveled, and I take most of the blame. Still, I couldn't help but wonder if my father's death had quietly frayed my ability to stay, to commit, to jump into the unknown of whether things could work out second-guessing myself.

Anyway, I digress.

What mattered was this: I wanted to see what would happen if I stopped steering altogether, if I let life handle the wheel.

After learning that selling frozen cheesecakes wasn't as lucrative as I thought, and after selling souvenirs at the $10 store off Hollywood Blvd. and ultimately working for my cousin at his design firm, I became a real estate agent. At this point I had just started closing some deals and finally had some decent money in my pocket. So, I bought a ticket to Thailand with no plan: no hotels booked, no research, and no idea how lost in translation I'd be. Just the curiosity and desire to go deeper into surrender, on purpose.

Just like watching the footage of my father dying in the World Trade Center over and over I didn't know what I was doing at first. I only knew I wanted to feel something real.

I got lost immediately. And I mean immediately. As soon as I stepped off the plane, I didn't even know how to get to the hostel in downtown Bangkok that I booked the night before leaving.

I turned left when I was supposed to right. I was scared to ask for help so I stayed disoriented longer than I had to only to learn help was on every corner. I let go of this egotistical feeling of having to figure out *everything* on my own. I felt self-conscious; I had to pull up what felt like false confidence to approach people I didn't know and to wander down streets I've never seen. All the while trusting my instincts and natural intuition we all have.

The first morning I ventured to the Grand Temple with thousands of other people. I happened to be there the same time the King of Thailand passed away so I was ironically swimming in the streets of mourning dressed in black. I felt a camaraderie. This was 15 years after my father's death so I wasn't in early grief but at the same time I felt like I was grieving who I was. Not because the only me was dying but because I was discovering a new me. Feeling as if for the first time I found the pulse of life that matched my heartbeat. Scared but still doing it. And, not fully certain what *it* even is. Maybe *it* is just life. I realized that getting lost might not be a failure; it might be the point.

This trip I communicated more with my hands than my mouth. Stumbled into places that no travel blog ever mentioned. And somehow, it all felt right.

I met a melting pot crew of travelers—people from every corner of the globe, all flying solo, no one knowing what the next five minutes would hold. I didn't come across a lot of Americans traveling solo. A nod to the way the west has everything completely discombobulated when it comes to living and the way the world flows. The belief the world stops only around borders. A lack of willingness to see what the rest of the world has to offer and that our differences aren't so vast. This isn't political. It's a philosophical observation of witnessing a lack of Americans in my travels willing to explore the rest of the world.

So, it goes.

Then I met Angel (Ahn-hel).

He was from Barcelona, staying in the same Chiang Mai hostel, frantically searching for his phone he never ended up finding (or replacing). We laughed at this mishap and a friendship began.

Off to the next city of Pai, I told him where I'd be and to look for me. If he found me great, if he didn't then good luck with his phone dilemma. By some Spanish grace of God he found me in the streets of Pai making his way to the hotel. Signifying the planned yet unplanned synchronicities that occur in life when we just let go of the outcome.

In Pai, we joined a group of travelers from every corner of the world the next day. We rented motorbikes and followed the winding roads up into the mountains. The air cooled as we climbed, my heart warmed as we rose. Every turn revealed a new slice of sky that we'd periodically stop to admire. With every foot of elevation I started feeling lighter (and heavier) with the realization that I was moving further from everything I'd known.

At the top, we roamed aimlessly, trusting strangers to lead the way and at times I led the way. They trusted me right back. Perhaps, it wasn't even trust. It was just a *let's see what happens; we'll figure it out.*

After some time at the peak of the mountain, I remembered I had laundry to pick up before the shop closed. Everyone laughed when I said I should go back not believing I'd make it in time. Staying would have been safer to stick with the pack nearly two hours away from the city center nearly touching the heavens. But something in me wanted to test what would happen if I followed my own pull, not logic. To not think about the worst-case scenario seeking the more likely outcome of safety.

I hopped on my motorbike and started down the mountain—racing the sunset, chasing the last gold light to clean linens. I shoved in my old, wired headphones and hit play on the only artist downloaded on my phone: U2.

The slow build of "Where the Streets Have No Name" filled my ears before I could determine which song it was. I pulled the throttle down an unpaved road and just ahead of cows crossed lazily in front of me. Their bells clanking in uneven rhythm completely on their own. I slowed to let them pass. The song was swelling as if moving with the cows—getting higher and louder as the last one cleared the path.

It was at that point I pulled the throttle back, sped as fast as I could, and let out a primal yell. I shouted the words into the wind to disperse into the hills once with me and now not. I was speeding up, feeling everything all at once where I couldn't tell if I wanted to cry or laugh.

Something inside me was being rewritten.

I sunk down the mountain through the golden haze of twilight with no map, one road to follow, and an odd sense of faith. And for those 90 minutes down the slope I felt realized I wasn't chasing anything anymore. I was just alive.

I made it back for my laundry—just barely—but I didn't want to stop there.

The night called and I followed it.

I followed the pull of the night to Pai Canyon—a popular place to hike up to the top that has a series of narrow, dirt trails with steep ass drop-offs on both sides—no rails, no real safety—just paths carved into a mountain. It's beautiful, a little sketchy, and the reason as to why it was empty when I arrived as the last one going up in the dark. Every step on that mountain was uncertain metaphorically and literally. Google Pai Canyon.

Against every ounce of rational sense and with every pound of testing myself, I hiked up alone under the dim, breathless sky. At the top, I crossed a narrow path of only a few feet bordered by a death drop on both sides.

Guided by the blanket of stars. I took a seat under the Asian moon, swarmed by silence and the kind of solitude that makes you forget anyone else exists for a moment.

That moment changed me.

I thought of my mother and my sisters 8,500 miles away. I was so far from everything I knew yet this moment was everything I wanted. I was alone and not alone. I was happy and sad. And, when those two merged it melted into peace. The balance of both. A perfect metaphor for living and grieving. They're not always mutually exclusive.

As I sat, I looked up to remember 8,500 miles is nothing compared to the cosmos. Tears fell from my eyes. The harmony of an invisible world so far from my family yet I've never felt so close. It was the first time I *felt* the truth I had only understood intellectually: that not knowing can be sacred and sometimes you're not supposed to do what you're supposed to do. That uncertainty, when embraced, can lead us somewhere deeper than any plan ever could.

I didn't chase the moment. I followed the uncertainty just to see where it went. And, if it didn't turn out the way I'd hoped or put me in danger, well, I'd worry about it then.

I've tried to live that way—never perfectly. But I try. I trust the unfolding. I trust my instincts. I trust that even when I don't know where I'm going—something in me does.

And above all, I trust this: it's all going to end. So, while I'm here, I'm going to live. And that living doesn't have to be flooring it on a motorbike after seeing Thai cows. As cinematic as this scene was to me—it's more in the small, quiet kind of living we do every single day.

Let the music play—even if you don't recognize the song. Because the point was never to know every move. Or, that everything we *should* do is what we could do.

The point is the dance.

THE MYTH OF "SUPPOSED TO"

When I was a kid, it felt like there was a rulebook to life. Parents, teachers, coaches, and, in general, authorities telling me how life is supposed to be lived. Even though you were just legally allowed to drive a car in public, you better start figuring out what you want to do *for the rest of your life*. Go to school, do this, do that.

By 12, I got the exact opposite message. My dad died in a terrorist attack with thousands others. He was here, and then he wasn't. He was supposed to stay longer. Supposed to watch me grow up. Supposed to be one of those old men in a recliner giving unsolicited advice and eating pretzels. Instead, he became a story I tell in the past tense.

Life doesn't go how it's "supposed to," most of the time.

You're supposed to be happy. You're supposed to fall in love and then have your heart broken, buy a house, maybe put up with a golden retriever that sheds way too much. You're supposed to live a long life. You're supposed to have your people for your whole life—or at the very least, for most of it. There's an order to things. A quiet little contract that none of us remembers signing.

It turns out, none of that is legally binding. No $25 notary. No lawyer. Just vague cultural osmosis and Hallmark cards. But we still treat it like a law of the universe—like gravity. And then life does what it does. And grief shows up. And the entire illusion shatters.

It's a fantasy we're all too scared to admit we're clinging to. And grief, bless its brutal honesty, doesn't ask our permission. It shows up with its sleeves rolled and says, "I'm sorry. We're doing this now. There will be no script. Good luck." It took me a while to stop being angry about that.

It's easy to think, "This wasn't supposed to happen to me."

But eventually, I had to ask the uncomfortable question, *Says who?*

Who promised me my dad would live until 85? Who promised anyone anything?

We talk about life like it's a train schedule. But it's more like a Ferris wheel. You don't know when your seat's going to stop at the top or when the operator's going to say, "Alright, folks, that's it." Sometimes you get the full ride. Sometimes you get off early because of rain. We're born into a culture that hands us instructions. If everyone grieves differently then it's likely that we should do exactly that. Grieve differently.

No one says that you might lose someone so early that the rest of your life is built on that absence. Maybe we could—not to build fear but to build gratefulness for the finite time that we have. A finite time where maybe *supposed to* is written in pencil and we don't have to know exactly what we're supposed to do because there is no *supposed*, only *possible*.

We are constantly adjusting to the loss of the life we thought we'd have. And that is its own kind of mourning. A grieving of a future neglected. The pain of what was supposed to be. Nobody throws you a funeral for that. There's no vegetable lasagna for the grief of not living the life you expected. But that grief is real. And it's everywhere. It's not just death. It's in the people who stayed in a marriage too long. Or never had a child. Or never finished the book. Or never got to say goodbye.

It's in the quiet moments. When you're brushing your teeth and realize the person you thought would be here forever is no longer brushing theirs. When you pass a photo with your loved one realizing you won't take another. When you go to text them and forget, for a second, that you can't.

Letting go of "supposed to" isn't giving up. This is an unshackling. A release of pressure to do things a certain way because of what our subconscious has absorbed or somebody told us. It's a reminder to make the most of every damn moment because what if we're not *supposed to* be here for a long time?

Life might not owe us anything. Not time. Not clarity. Not equality of outcome. And death doesn't follow our rules. It doesn't wait for the birthday party to end or for the reconciliation to happen. It comes mid-conversation, mid-laugh, mid-fight. It can be rude like that.

The older I get, the more I realize that most of our suffering isn't from what happens—it's from the gap between what happened and what we thought *should* happen.

We're not just grieving the death. We're grieving the wedding he was supposed to attend. The road trip that never happened. The someday that vanished. And, the reverse, we can grieve the things we were supposed to do when that person was alive.

But there's also a strange peace that comes when you stop expecting the universe to follow your plan.

The moment you surrender *supposed to,* you get access to what *is*.

You start noticing weird things. Like the way two flight attendants work together to organize an overbooked flight while you wait to board. Or how laughter can show up in the middle of a hospital waiting room. How our darkest moments can enhance the visibility of light no matter how small it looks. It's not that things become easy. It's just that they stop needing to be.

I know people who think they're behind in life. In fact, I'm in that group from time to time. Then I think, *Behind what? Who is running this race? The tortoise?*

I've met people who say, "I thought I'd have it all figured out by now." As if figuring it out is even a real thing. I've talked to 80-year-olds who still don't know what they want to be when they grow up.

And, to me, that's okay. Being human isn't about achieving some final form. Author Earl Nightingale said, "Success is the progressive realization of a worthy goal or ideal." And I think we can replace the word *success* with *living*.

That quote doesn't mention how much we have in the bank when we die. We treat success like it's a finish line. And we do the same with life. My interpretation is that it's the *journey*. The journey toward something that matters *to you*.

Progressive realization is the movement, not the finish line. It doesn't matter if you're moving fast, slow, or both at times. It just means moving toward something meaningful regardless of the outcome. Then you are already living in success.

It's not the achievement, the dusty trophies on the shelf. It's the direction, effort, and alignment in doing something meaningful no matter how big or how small society may deem it.

And your goals should align with who you are and what improves your life or others around you. What stretches you into discomfort that you would pursue whether you got the praise for it, or not.

My father didn't get to grow old. He didn't get the ole' slow fade. He got a hard stop. But he loved. He showed up. He smoked cigars and said his sacred mantra "hey, kid" that I have tatted on my body. That mattered.

He didn't finish the ride like we're *supposed* to. But he rode it well. And maybe that's what we're supposed to do.

The moment you accept that you stop fighting the wrong battle. You grieve, yes. But you also live. You stumble into beauty you weren't looking for. You meet people you never planned to meet. You fall apart and rebuild. You grow, and sometimes, you laugh at the absurdity of it all.

So, it goes.

Sometimes, the only way to find faith is to get lost on purpose.

I still hear that U2 song sometimes. It reminds me not of the ride itself but of the moment I stopped trying to know where I was going, wondering if I should and let go of where I'll end up. Because maybe that's what living really is—trusting the road, even when the street has no name.

CONCLUSION
HEY, KID

"He brought life into a room. That's just who he was."
—Uncle Augie, Episode 235

Dad, I think of you all the time.

When I look at grainy family videos it reminds me that I've spent more than half my life without you and none of my adult life with you.

I can't help but think what man to man could have been like. You only knew me as a boy. And I only knew you from a boy's eyes. Now as a man our conversations have been left to my imagination. It's interesting how the waves of emotion I still get aren't rooted in sadness. I've created a simplified outlook on life. Your death made me grow up.

It made me love harder. Now I look a little longer at the people I love. I'll stay a little longer. Not freed from the human moments of distraction yet filled with moments of being aware of my distractions. Because the fragility of life was exposed to me at a young age; your absence taught me what truly matters. Yet, at the same time you've never felt truly absent.

I think about you all the time and that keeps you with me. I often reflect on how my father's death—an existential sacrifice I didn't ask for—led me toward a fuller life, deeper understanding, and a path that has become this work. Because I wonder if you could have taught me as much as you have if you were alive.

Regardless of any lessons I learned from that day I would trade every one of them just to have you back. I'd grab that nonexistent grief receipt and return the whole thing if it meant I could have you here as a father, not a memory. But grief has a strict no-return policy.

What still breaks me is still seeing Mom's watery eyes when we have our deep talks. Or catching the way my sisters drift into their own quiet of missing you when we find ourselves sharing those moments. But even those tears have changed meaning for me. They're not just sadness—they're love. And if there wasn't contrast, if life didn't strike with thunder and clear skies, none of this would feel as profound as it does.

As heavy as it all can be, your absence somehow made life feel lighter. Not easier—just clearer. You showed me, even in dying, what truly matters. You taught me after death comes life.

I remember the day you dropped me off to elementary school once. You shouted my name from the car for no reason except to have some fun. As I stepped into the front door of my school, I still heard you yelling my name intentionally causing an innocent scene. I was mortified as an inexperienced ignorant child. Embarrassed to the point where I didn't want you to drop me off at school again. Now looking back, I would live that moment for eternity if I could. I'd ask to feel the eternal illusion of embarrassment if it meant I could feel your voice on the back of my neck as I walked away.

It's funny how grief sends you back to the past with new eyes. The future I thought was taken from me wasn't really taken—it was just rewritten. Because we never *have* the future. What used to feel sad now feels like perspective. The tears I've cried over you aren't just grief; they're all the love we shared and still have, all the things I wish we got to do, and the reminder that this life is fragile and incredible all at once.

Death and life are two sides of the same coin. And because of you I recognize the beauty of life.

It's just one big dark comedy. To not take it too seriously and live shamelessly authentic. I'd be doing you a disservice if I didn't live life to my definition of the fullest. It just took time to realize that I didn't have to rush.

Now as a man, I still have days where "full" feels different than it used to. I wish you knew me now. I wish I could hear you say you're proud of me. I even wish I could hear you tell me when you're disappointed. I still want your advice and your voice that's not played from a family video. But even without that, I can feel you in quieter ways—in my intuition and my choices the footprint you left guides every step I take.

I am living now in the future that I grieved as a boy. I'll never get to hear your stories that you can only tell your son when he's old enough. I won't hear the stories you had roaming around as a young buck before you met my mother. But I am blessed to hear these stories from the bullpen of relievers I have ready to finish the game you were taken out of.

I'm comfortable at this point of my life with my grief. Time has done a number on my memory and I have put a lot of effort into evolving and dancing with grief to become the person I am today: an imperfect man continually learning and looking back to that fateful day. Loosening my grip on choices avoided and choices made. There isn't a day that goes by where I don't yearn to have you by my side. I want to ask you for advice. I want to just sit in silence as we watch the ball game. I want to be able to call you and ask if you want to go grab a beer.

Some days I accept this reality, and some days I don't. I used to force myself into acceptance because I thought that's what "healing" meant. Now I know it's okay to have days where it still sucks. The key is just not living there too long. Acceptance isn't a finish line—it's a messy, human rhythm.

It's the *staying in there too long* that can throw us down a spiral. The art of acceptance is an elegant cluster fuck of ups and downs. And that's okay. I find it comical to accept the fact that there are some days I don't want to accept it. Just another wonderful example of the oxymoron that is grief.

But I thank you for still teaching me.

It's always the little things that echo the loudest.

THE LITTLE THINGS

In the grand tapestry of existence, it's often the small, underdressed moments that weave the most profound threads into the fabric of our lives. Often the routine moments that can easily be taken for granted.

The way my buddy Jake and I have spontaneous hour-long conversations that have no direction. When I get the first hug from my mother or sisters when I come back to visit New Jersey. That cool breeze that pokes its head on a hot day and for those few seconds you feel like you're in a Winterfresh Gum commercial. The way the clouds cover up the sun for a moment building up a reveal to this fiery star in the distance. A text message from my best friend just to say hi and most likely make fun of me.

These are the little moments that hold immense significance, and it took time to realize the importance of noticing those moments *while we're in them*. Because to notice those moments while we're in them it requires presence. It requires slowing things down. Cascading our focus to one thing: the moment.

They serve as gentle reminders that amidst chaos, there is tranquility, amidst uncertainty, there is hope. And a realization of what we have right now. I know it's much easier said than done. This life is difficult.

Our struggles are real. Which is why I like shrinking our focus to the little things in life.

At the same time, I'm not training to be a superhero monk here. There are going to be moments I'm not present and that's okay. But I do strive to continually be more and more present.

My family left an everlasting imprint of what unconditional love truly means. And it's my father who possessed a remarkable ability to find joy and peace in the simplest of pleasures, teaching me that happiness isn't found in grand gestures or extravagant pursuits, but rather in the quiet moments of everyday life.

One of my favorite memories of my father is watching my dad pluck weeds from the yard. I used to think he was out of his mind. Now I understand—it was presence. It was pride. It was the little things he cared for, just like he cared for us. I feel that same presence now when I catch myself appreciating moments I would've ignored years ago. And that's the trade-off between the mark he left unable to verbalize what he may have wanted to teach me. Now I learn through memory and lessons only his death taught me.

In those moments, I learned that true happiness comes not from the magnitude of action, but from the mindfulness and presence with which it is carried out. And the importance of recognizing those moments while you're in them. When I find myself in that bubble I vibrate with gratefulness that just at the bare minimum just for a moment things feel okay.

Being present is a practice, and noticing life's little signals has become my way of staying connected to him and the people in my life. The way he enjoyed every meal and the way he intentionally farted in a room we were all trapped in was his expression of love and what is truly important. Those are the little things I miss the most. Now today it's made me so grateful for the seemingly routine things in life that often get overlooked among the daily distractions from our phone, bills, our jobs or the constant berating of divisiveness this world seems to be promoting. We're all grazing this weird little world together and every day share these little things in harmony, sometimes we just don't see it.

One time a stranger yelled at me about wild parrots flying overhead—something I didn't even know existed in Los Angeles. Her excitement made me look up. That moment with a stranger mattered to me in a way it probably wouldn't have years ago. That's what grief does—it sharpens your awareness of connection and trying to see things from other vantage points.

Though my father may no longer be physically present, he's with me all the time because of the little things in life. Not in what's considered modern day success but the compassion I try to exude among my family, friends, and humans I may never see again. Whether it's the laughter of loved ones or the gust of a wind that seems to rejuvenate my soul, I am reminded that life's greatest treasures are often found in the smallest moments. And in those moments, I find solace, knowing that no matter what challenges may come my way, everything will be okay.

This experience taught me that pain isn't the enemy—it's part of the curriculum. Life tests us, but it also reveals us. I've been blessed, and I carry a heavy heart for those suffering, but I can only speak from my own path and where it's led me.

It's ironic how the purest form of pain shines light on the purest form of love. And, if it wasn't for my dad dying, I may never have shed the veil of the matrix that has allowed me to *feel* life. I'm grateful.

The pain sucks. But on another side of it I'm grateful for it. I'm grateful for the moments of uncertainty that are perpetual as I continue on. Life's tests make sense to me now because life is just a classroom.

I've been blessed all the way through my life. I wear a heavy heart to all those suffering more than I am. I can only speak from my experiences and how I decipher the code thrust on me onto my soul. It's up to you to do it for yourself and your important little world.

I just know that the next time life throws me a knuckle sandwich I'll embrace it with open arms.

Not because I'm happy that it's happening but because I know this is how it goes. I know now that my spirit can only be broken if I choose it to be.

My dad's death has tried to define my life. And instead, I decided to define it myself.

I believe my father is still around me, and that I'll see him again—maybe not wearing shorts in 30-degree weather like he would here, but in some form I'll instantly recognize. When that moment comes, I won't need proof. I'll just know.

If it happens, when it happens, whenever it happens, I'll stay ready to greet him with one more, "Hey, kid."

A photo of my father and me in Fire Island, New York, sometime in the 90's.

ACKNOWLEDGMENTS

There are too many people in my life to acknowledge.

And, there is only one person to start with.

My mother is my hero. Even to this day all the way down to the minute details she has laid a foundation that is unbreakable. She taught me what love is. True unconditional love that has made me question the societal stigma that there is no such thing as a selfless act.

She's the epitome of expressing the gentleness of a dragonfly and the strength of a warrior. The balance of both has made me compassionate, loving and fueled to withstand anything in life. Her strength carries more people in this world than she'd admit. I'll have to contact Webster's Dictionary to create a new word that explains all that she is because the words don't exist to honor this woman.

This all trickled down to my sisters who are my rocks. There's nothing they wouldn't do for me and in turn I can say the same for them. Just like my mother, everything that is good in me down to my atoms comes from my beautiful sisters. Their strength, their willingness to step in the line of fire for the benefit of my life is indescribable.

They taught me to see life differently and that no matter what missteps I take I know that they are there. We've been through hell, and when they get scorched by the flames so do I. The scars we all hold are unique to each of us but they come from some of the same battles. We may be bound in blood without the choice of who my siblings are but if I was to be given the choice to choose—there is no other option. They're my everything and my why.

Then there's those I do not share the same bloodline with who have become family through experiential transfusion. My loyal best friend, James, who unironically was the one who walked beside me that day on September 11 before everything flipped upside down. The way he'd step on a sword for me defines what real friendship and support means. The entirety of my little league baseball team from the parents all the way down to each kid whom I still remain close with today. They showed me how people can rally together selflessly only to express how important community can be. And how a community should be seen as a whole but to remember that it's made of selfless individuals.

This experience of losing a father gave me a brother. My sister's husband Jeff. They were destined to get married regardless but he showed up in our darkest times along with his entire family. He was just a young man in college at that time and still chose to be by our side day in and day out. It's the people in your life whom you not only share the best times with but also the worst. And my *brother* Jeff is that.

My mother's partner Ken, who fell in love with my mom a few years after September 11 and has become another father figure. He stepped into an uncomfortable situation knowing he would never replace my father and he has never tried. He's given our family and my mother the love I know he'd want for her.

Then there's what I thought was impossible. The opportunity for new memories. My dad's best friend and my Uncle Augie are extensions of my father through stories, guidance, and support. We've only gotten closer as I've grown into my own. He's been a consigliere to my family and another not tied by blood yet we'd give our blood for one another.

From cousins, aunts and uncles, friends and overall, the community of Middletown, New Jersey. And it continues to this day from the same people and new people in my life. I learned the lesson of relationships and the people in our lives cannot fully carry the burden for us, nor should they, but every now and then when the barbell in the gym of life falls flat on our chest it's vital to have a spotter that's there to help you lift the weight up when it gets too heavy.

The beautiful, strange odyssey from the events of September 11 is the way New York, the people in my community, and the nation did rally together. I used to think it was a shame how it can take tragedy to show what really matters in life. Now I think that, in part, is how it all works. It took tragedy for me to not take anything else for granted moving forward. It took tragedy to show our true colors and gave us the ability to color a different shade for the colors we don't like in ourselves. It was the adversity that became our lotus flower blossoming from the swamp.

Support comes in many forms. It doesn't have to be 50 people. It can just be one. Sometimes it's not even a person.

I've felt guilt at times for having the safety net that I've had. But I'm grateful for every person who stepped into the fire with us.

I can write an entire book in itself from the rest of my family and friends. You know who you are so don't get mad that your name isn't mentioned because I promise you your name is stamped on my heart.

And a quick shoutout to Linkin Park and Pearl Jam—they were therapy before I knew what therapy was.

I'd like to think these people know I would do the same for them and in some way I hope I've proven that.

In the words of Martin Luther King Jr., "If a man has not discovered something that he will die for, he isn't fit to live."

If there's one thing I do know for sure thanks to all the people in my life. It's that I must be fit to live.

ABOUT THE AUTHOR

David Ferrugio is the creator and host of *DEAD Talks*, a long-form podcast dedicated to honest, human conversations about death, grief, loss, and what it means to live well in the face of impermanence. Through hundreds of interviews with artists, thinkers, scientists, spiritual leaders, and everyday people, his work explores how confronting mortality can deepen meaning, connection, and purpose.

Ferrugio's path to this work is deeply personal. At the age of 12, he lost his father in the September 11 attacks—an experience that quietly shaped his relationship with grief, identity, and the unanswered questions we carry through life. Years later, those questions became the foundation for *DEAD Talks* and for his writing: not to offer certainty, but to create space for reflection, humor, discomfort, and shared humanity.

His approach is grounded, curious, and accessible, blending personal storytelling with cultural observation and philosophical insight. Rather than treating grief as something to "get over," Ferrugio invites readers to see it as something that can coexist with joy, growth, and a fully lived life.

This book marks his debut as an author and extends the core mission of *DEAD Talks*: to normalize conversations about death, challenge our assumptions about grief, and remind us that paying attention to our mortality can make us more alive.

David Ferrugio was born in Staten Island, New York, and raised in New Jersey.